SWISS COOKBOOK

Traditional Authentic Recipes from Switzerland

LIAM LUXE

Copyright © 2023 Liam Luxe

All rights reserved.

CONTENTS

APPETIZERS 1
    Traditional Swiss Cheese Fondue 1
    Swiss Rösti 2
    Zürcher Geschnetzeltes (Zurich-Style Sliced Veal) 3
    Maluns (Swiss Potato Dish) 4
    Swiss Onion Soup 5
    Chäschüechli (Swiss Cheese Tart) 6
    Swiss Chard and Cheese Tart 7
    Walliser Käseschnitte (Valaisian Cheese Toast) 8

SOUPS AND SALADS 10
    Minestrone alla Svizzera (Swiss Minestrone) 10
    Swiss Potato Leek Soup 11
    Nüsslisalat (Swiss Nut Salad) 12
    Swiss Beetroot Salad 13
    Birchermüesli (Swiss Muesli) 14
    Swiss Green Bean Salad 15
    Swiss Cucumber Salad 16

MAIN DISHES 17
    Zürcher Eintopf (Zurich Hotpot) 17
    Raclette 18
    Swiss Meatloaf (Hackbraten) 19
    Swiss Bratwurst with Rösti 20
    Bernerplatte (Bernese Platter) 22

Swiss Chicken Cordon Bleu 23
Swiss Beef Stroganoff 24
Swiss Chicken Fricassee 25
Swiss Cheese and Onion Quiche 26

SIDE DISHES 28
Alplermagronen (Swiss Alpine Macaroni) 28
Swiss Spätzli 29
Swiss Red Cabbage 30
Swiss Creamed Spinach 31
Swiss Glace de Viande (Gravy) 32
Swiss Vegetable Gratin 33
Swiss Sweet Potato Gratin 34

BREADS AND PASTRIES 37
Swiss Zopf (Braided Bread) 37
Swiss Rüeblitorte (Carrot Cake) 38
Nusstorte (Swiss Nut Tart) 40
Swiss Biberli (Honey-Glazed Cookies) 42
Basler Läckerli (Swiss Gingerbread) 44
Zuger Kirschtorte (Cherry Cake) 45
Swiss Butterzopf 48
Swiss Chocolate Mousse Cake 49

CHEESE DISHES 53
Cheese Slices (Käseschnitten) 53
Swiss Cheese and Herb Pancakes 54
Cheese and Potato Dumplings 56
Swiss Cheese Gnocchi 58

Swiss Cheese and Onion Soup 60
Swiss Cheese Stuffed Mushrooms 61
Cheese and Spinach Stuffed Chicken 63

VEGETARIAN DISHES 66
Swiss Cheese and Mushroom Risotto 66
Swiss Cheese and Spinach Quiche 68
Swiss Chard and Potato Gratin 70
Cheese-Stuffed Peppers 72
Swiss Cheese and Vegetable Tart 73
Swiss Cheese and Potato Bake 75

DESSERTS 77
Swiss Chocolate Fondue 77
Nusstorte (Nut Cake) 78
Swiss Plum Tart 80
Swiss Lemon Tart 82
Engadiner Nusstorte (Nut Tart from Engadin) 84
Swiss Apple Strudel 86
Swiss Chocolate Truffles 88
Swiss Meringue 89
Swiss Nut Pralines 90

BREAKFAST AND BRUNCH 92
Rüeblitorte (Carrot Cake) Pancakes 92
Swiss Bircher Muesli Bowl 94
Swiss Chocolate Croissants 95
Swiss Cheese Breakfast Quiche 96
Swiss Potato Breakfast Hash 98

Swiss Fruit and Yogurt Parfait 99
GRILLED AND ROASTED 101
   Swiss Grilled Chicken 101
   Swiss Roasted Pork 102
   Swiss Grilled Trout 104
   Grilled Swiss Sausages 105
   Swiss Roast Beef 106
   Swiss Roasted Lamb 107
PASTA AND RICE 110
   Swiss Cheese Pasta 110
   Swiss Cheese Risotto 111
   Swiss Cheese and Mushroom Pasta 112
   Swiss Cheese and Ham Pasta 113
   Swiss Rice Pudding 114
   Swiss Rice and Vegetable Pilaf 116
SNACKS AND FINGER FOODS 118
   Swiss Cheese Bites 118
   Swiss Cheese and Ham Bites 119
   Swiss Cheese Straws 120
   Swiss Roasted Nuts 121
   Swiss Cheese and Tomato Skewers 122
   Swiss Cheese and Onion Tartlets 123
   Swiss Cheese Stuffed Peppers 125
SWEETS AND TREATS 127
   Swiss Chocolate Brownies 127
   Swiss Fruit Compote 128

Swiss Apple Crumble 129

Swiss Caramel Pudding 131

Swiss Hazelnut Brittle 133

Swiss Meringue Cookies 134

Swiss Nut Brittle 135

Swiss Chocolate Hazelnut Spread 137

HOLIDAY SPECIALS 139

Swiss Christmas Cookies 139

Swiss Easter Bread 141

Swiss Cheese Fondue for New Year's 143

Swiss Thanksgiving Pie 145

Swiss Hanukkah Latkes 147

Swiss Valentine's Chocolate Fondue 148

MEASUREMENT CONVERSIONS 150

INTRODUCTION

This book is all about Swiss food, and it has over 100 easy-to-make recipes that show you how to cook delicious Swiss dishes. Swiss food is not just about famous things like Swiss chocolate and cheese. It's a mix of flavors from different parts of Switzerland, and it's really tasty. From cheesy dishes to yummy desserts, this cookbook has it all.

Whether you're an experienced cook or just starting out, these recipes are designed to help you make Swiss food at home. Each step is explained clearly, so you can follow along easily.

Swiss people love using fresh ingredients from their beautiful country. As you cook these recipes, you'll discover how important nature and tradition are to Swiss cooking.

You don't need to be in Switzerland to enjoy Swiss food. You can make these dishes in your own kitchen and share them with your family and friends. It's a fun way to explore a new culture through food.

APPETIZERS

TRADITIONAL SWISS CHEESE FONDUE

Servings: 4 **Time:** 30 minutes

Ingredients:

- 1 clove garlic
- 1 1/2 cups (175g) Gruyère cheese, grated
- 1 1/2 cups (175g) Emmental cheese, grated
- 1 cup (240ml) dry white wine
- 1 tablespoon cornstarch
- 1 teaspoon lemon juice
- A pinch of nutmeg
- A pinch of white pepper
- 1 loaf of French bread, cubed

Instructions:

1. Rub the inside of a fondue pot with the garlic clove, then discard the garlic.
2. In a bowl, combine the grated Gruyère and Emmental cheese with cornstarch. Toss to coat the cheese evenly.
3. Pour the white wine and lemon juice into the fondue pot and heat over medium-low heat until it's hot but not boiling.
4. Gradually add the cheese mixture to the pot, stirring constantly in a figure-eight motion until the cheese melts and the mixture becomes smooth.
5. Season with nutmeg and white pepper. Stir well.
6. Serve immediately with the cubed French bread for dipping. Use long-stemmed forks to spear the bread and dip it in the melted cheese.

SWISS RÖSTI

Servings: 4 **Time:** 30 minutes

Ingredients:

- 4 large potatoes, peeled and grated
- 2 tablespoons butter
- 2 tablespoons vegetable oil
- Salt and pepper to taste

Instructions:

1. Grate the peeled potatoes into a clean kitchen towel, then squeeze out any excess moisture.

2. In a large non-stick skillet, heat the butter and vegetable oil over medium-high heat.
3. Add the grated potatoes to the hot pan, spreading them out evenly.
4. Press the potatoes down with a spatula to form a flat cake. Season with salt and pepper.
5. Cook for about 10-15 minutes or until the bottom is golden and crispy.
6. Carefully flip the Rösti using a large plate or lid, and cook the other side until it's golden and crispy as well.
7. Once both sides are golden and the potatoes are tender, slide the Rösti onto a plate.
8. Cut into wedges and serve hot. It's delicious as a side dish for breakfast or any meal.

ZÜRCHER GESCHNETZELTES (ZURICH-STYLE SLICED VEAL)

Servings: 4 **Time:** 30 minutes

Ingredients:

- 1 pound (450g) veal, thinly sliced into strips
- 2 tablespoons butter
- 1 small onion, finely chopped
- 1/2 cup (120ml) white wine
- 1/2 cup (120ml) heavy cream
- 1 tablespoon all-purpose flour
- 1 tablespoon lemon juice
- 2 tablespoons fresh parsley, chopped
- Salt and pepper to taste

Instructions:

1. In a large skillet, melt the butter over medium-high heat.
2. Add the veal strips and cook for 2-3 minutes until they are no longer pink. Remove the veal from the skillet and set it aside.
3. In the same skillet, add the chopped onion and cook until it becomes translucent.
4. Sprinkle the flour over the onions and stir for a minute to create a roux.
5. Pour in the white wine, stirring to make a smooth sauce.
6. Add the heavy cream, lemon juice, and return the cooked veal to the skillet. Stir well.
7. Let the mixture simmer for a few minutes until the sauce thickens.
8. Season with salt and pepper, and sprinkle with fresh parsley.
9. Serve hot over cooked egg noodles or rice.

MALUNS (SWISS POTATO DISH)

Servings: 4 **Time:** 40 minutes

Ingredients:

- 4 large potatoes, peeled and thinly sliced
- 2 tablespoons butter
- 1 tablespoon sugar
- 1/2 teaspoon salt
- 1/2 teaspoon ground cinnamon
- 1/4 cup (60ml) milk

Instructions:

1. In a large skillet, melt the butter over medium heat.
2. Add the thinly sliced potatoes and cook for about 10-15 minutes, or until they start to brown and become tender.
3. Sprinkle the sugar, salt, and ground cinnamon over the potatoes. Stir to coat them evenly.
4. Reduce the heat to low, pour in the milk, and let the potatoes simmer for another 10-15 minutes, or until they are soft and caramelized.
5. Serve your Maluns hot as a side dish or even with applesauce for a sweet twist.

SWISS ONION SOUP

Servings: 4 **Time:** 45 minutes

Ingredients:

- 4 large onions, thinly sliced
- 2 tablespoons butter
- 6 cups (1.5 liters) beef or vegetable broth
- 2 slices of Swiss cheese
- 4 slices of crusty bread
- Salt and pepper to taste

Instructions:

1. In a large pot, melt the butter over medium heat.
2. Add the thinly sliced onions and cook for about 20-25 minutes, or until they are soft and caramelized.
3. Pour in the beef or vegetable broth and bring the soup to a simmer. Let it cook for an additional 10 minutes.
4. Season with salt and pepper to taste.

5. Preheat your oven's broiler.
6. Ladle the hot soup into oven-safe bowls.
7. Place a slice of bread on top of each bowl and cover it with a slice of Swiss cheese.
8. Put the bowls under the broiler for a few minutes, or until the cheese is bubbly and golden brown.
9. Serve your Swiss Onion Soup hot, being careful not to touch the hot bowls.

CHÄSCHÜECHLI (SWISS CHEESE TART)

Servings: 8 **Time:** 40 minutes

Ingredients:

- 1 pre-made pie crust (9-inch)
- 2 cups (200g) Swiss cheese, grated (Emmental or Gruyère)
- 1/2 cup (120ml) heavy cream
- 2 large eggs
- 1/4 teaspoon nutmeg
- Salt and pepper to taste

Instructions:

1. Preheat your oven to 375°F (190°C).
2. Place the pre-made pie crust in a 9-inch pie dish and prick the bottom with a fork.
3. In a bowl, combine the grated Swiss cheese, heavy cream, eggs, nutmeg, salt, and pepper. Mix until well combined.
4. Pour the cheese mixture into the pie crust.

5. Bake in the preheated oven for about 25-30 minutes, or until the tart is set and the top is golden brown.
6. Allow it to cool for a few minutes before slicing.

SWISS CHARD AND CHEESE TART

Servings: 6 **Time:** 50 minutes

Ingredients:

- 1 pre-made pie crust (9-inch)
- 1 bunch Swiss chard, stems removed and leaves chopped
- 1 cup (100g) Swiss cheese, grated (Emmental or Gruyère)
- 3 large eggs
- 1 cup (240ml) milk
- Salt and pepper to taste
- A pinch of nutmeg

Instructions:

1. Preheat your oven to 375°F (190°C).
2. Place the pre-made pie crust in a 9-inch pie dish and prick the bottom with a fork.
3. In a large skillet, sauté the chopped Swiss chard until it wilts and any excess moisture evaporates. Season with salt and pepper.
4. Spread the sautéed Swiss chard and grated Swiss cheese evenly in the pie crust.
5. In a bowl, whisk together the eggs, milk, a pinch of nutmeg, salt, and pepper.

6. Pour the egg mixture over the Swiss chard and cheese in the pie crust.
7. Bake in the preheated oven for about 30-35 minutes, or until the tart is set and the top is golden.
8. Let it cool for a few minutes before slicing.

WALLISER KÄSESCHNITTE (VALAISIAN CHEESE TOAST)

Servings: 4 **Time:** 20 minutes

Ingredients:

- 4 slices of rustic bread
- 2 cups (200g) Swiss cheese, grated (Emmental or Gruyère)
- 1/2 cup (120ml) white wine
- 2 cloves garlic, minced
- A pinch of nutmeg
- Salt and pepper to taste
- 2 tablespoons butter

Instructions:

1. In a saucepan, melt the butter over medium heat.
2. Add the minced garlic and sauté for a minute until fragrant.
3. Pour in the white wine and bring it to a gentle simmer.
4. Add the grated Swiss cheese to the wine, stirring until it's melted and forms a smooth cheese sauce.
5. Season with a pinch of nutmeg, salt, and pepper to taste.

6. Toast the slices of rustic bread until they are lightly browned.
7. Pour the cheese sauce over the toasted bread slices.
8. Place the cheesy bread under a broiler for a few minutes until it's bubbly and golden brown.
9. Serve your Valaisian Cheese Toast hot.

SOUPS AND SALADS

MINESTRONE ALLA SVIZZERA (SWISS MINESTRONE)

Servings: 6 **Time:** 45 minutes

Ingredients:

- 1 tablespoon olive oil
- 1 onion, finely chopped
- 2 carrots, diced
- 2 celery stalks, diced
- 2 cloves garlic, minced
- 1 zucchini, diced
- 1 cup (200g) green beans, chopped
- 1 can (14 oz) diced tomatoes
- 4 cups (1 liter) vegetable broth

- 1 cup (100g) small pasta (such as elbow macaroni)
- 1 can (15 oz) white beans, drained and rinsed
- 2 cups (200g) Swiss chard, chopped
- Salt and pepper to taste
- Grated Parmesan cheese for serving

Instructions:

1. In a large pot, heat the olive oil over medium heat.
2. Add the chopped onion, carrots, celery, and garlic. Sauté until the vegetables are tender.
3. Stir in the zucchini and green beans and cook for a few more minutes.
4. Add the diced tomatoes and vegetable broth to the pot. Bring to a boil.
5. Stir in the small pasta and cook according to the pasta's package instructions.
6. Once the pasta is cooked, add the white beans and Swiss chard.
7. Let the soup simmer for a few minutes until the Swiss chard wilts.
8. Season with salt and pepper to taste.
9. Serve your Swiss Minestrone hot, with a sprinkle of grated Parmesan cheese on top.

SWISS POTATO LEEK SOUP

Servings: 4 **Time:** 30 minutes

Ingredients:

- 2 leeks, white and light green parts, sliced
- 4 cups (1 liter) vegetable or chicken broth

- 4 large potatoes, peeled and diced
- 2 tablespoons butter
- Salt and pepper to taste
- 1 cup (240ml) heavy cream (optional for a creamier soup)
- Chopped fresh chives for garnish (optional)

Instructions:

1. In a large pot, melt the butter over medium heat.
2. Add the sliced leeks and cook until they become soft and translucent.
3. Add the diced potatoes to the pot and pour in the vegetable or chicken broth.
4. Season with salt and pepper to taste.
5. Bring the soup to a boil, then reduce the heat and let it simmer for about 20-25 minutes, or until the potatoes are tender.
6. If you prefer a creamier soup, stir in the heavy cream.
7. Use an immersion blender to puree the soup until it reaches your desired consistency. You can also leave some chunks if you like it rustic.
8. Serve your Swiss Potato Leek Soup hot, and garnish with chopped fresh chives if desired.

NÜSSLISALAT (SWISS NUT SALAD)

Servings: 4 **Time:** 15 minutes

Ingredients:

- 4 cups (400g) lamb's lettuce (Nüsslisalat)
- 1/2 cup (50g) walnuts, roughly chopped

- 1/2 cup (50g) grated Swiss cheese (Emmental or Gruyère)
- 2 tablespoons olive oil
- 1 tablespoon white wine vinegar
- Salt and pepper to taste

Instructions:

1. Wash and dry the lamb's lettuce and place it in a large salad bowl.
2. Sprinkle the chopped walnuts and grated Swiss cheese over the lettuce.
3. In a small bowl, whisk together the olive oil, white wine vinegar, salt, and pepper to make the dressing.
4. Drizzle the dressing over the salad.
5. Toss the salad gently to coat the ingredients with the dressing.
6. Serve your Swiss Nut Salad immediately as a refreshing side dish.

SWISS BEETROOT SALAD

Servings: 4 **Time:** 30 minutes

Ingredients:

- 4 medium-sized beetroots, cooked, peeled, and diced
- 1/2 cup (120ml) sour cream or Greek yogurt
- 2 tablespoons horseradish
- 1 tablespoon lemon juice
- Salt and pepper to taste
- Fresh dill for garnish (optional)

Instructions:

1. In a large bowl, combine the diced cooked beetroots.
2. In a separate bowl, mix the sour cream or Greek yogurt with horseradish and lemon juice.
3. Season the dressing with salt and pepper to taste.
4. Pour the dressing over the beetroots and gently toss to coat them evenly.
5. If desired, garnish with fresh dill.

BIRCHERMÜESLI (SWISS MUESLI)

Servings: 2 **Time:** 10 minutes

Ingredients:

- 1 cup (90g) rolled oats
- 1/2 cup (120ml) plain yogurt
- 1/2 cup (120ml) milk
- 1 apple, grated
- 1/4 cup (30g) mixed nuts (e.g., almonds, hazelnuts), chopped
- 1/4 cup (30g) dried fruit (e.g., raisins, apricots), chopped
- 1 tablespoon honey
- Fresh berries or fruit for topping (optional)

Instructions:

1. In a bowl, combine the rolled oats, plain yogurt, and milk.
2. Add the grated apple, mixed nuts, and dried fruit to the mixture.

3. Drizzle with honey for sweetness.
4. Stir everything well to combine.
5. If desired, top with fresh berries or more fruit.

SWISS GREEN BEAN SALAD

Servings: 4 **Time:** 20 minutes

Ingredients:

- 1 pound (450g) green beans, trimmed and halved
- 1/4 cup (60ml) olive oil
- 2 tablespoons white wine vinegar
- 1 teaspoon Dijon mustard
- 2 cloves garlic, minced
- 1/4 cup (30g) red onion, finely chopped
- Salt and pepper to taste
- 1/4 cup (30g) fresh parsley, chopped

Instructions:

1. Bring a large pot of salted water to a boil. Add the green beans and cook for about 3-4 minutes, or until they are crisp-tender. Drain and transfer to a bowl of ice water to cool down. Drain again.
2. In a small bowl, whisk together the olive oil, white wine vinegar, Dijon mustard, minced garlic, red onion, salt, and pepper to make the dressing.
3. Place the green beans in a serving bowl and pour the dressing over them.
4. Toss to coat the green beans with the dressing.
5. Sprinkle the chopped fresh parsley over the salad.

6. Serve your Swiss Green Bean Salad chilled as a refreshing side dish.

SWISS CUCUMBER SALAD

Servings: 4 **Time:** 15 minutes

Ingredients:

- 2 cucumbers, thinly sliced
- 1/2 cup (120ml) sour cream
- 2 tablespoons white wine vinegar
- 1 tablespoon fresh dill, chopped
- 1 teaspoon sugar
- Salt and pepper to taste

Instructions:

1. In a large bowl, combine the thinly sliced cucumbers.
2. In a separate bowl, mix the sour cream, white wine vinegar, fresh dill, sugar, salt, and pepper to create the dressing.
3. Pour the dressing over the cucumbers and toss to coat them evenly.
4. Chill the salad in the refrigerator for at least 10 minutes before serving.
5. Serve your Swiss Cucumber Salad cold as a crisp and tangy side dish.

MAIN DISHES

ZÜRCHER EINTOPF (ZURICH HOTPOT)

Servings: 6 **Time:** 2 hours

Ingredients:

- 1 pound (450g) stewing beef, cut into chunks
- 4 sausages (such as cervelat or bratwurst), sliced
- 1 onion, chopped
- 2 cloves garlic, minced
- 4 large potatoes, peeled and diced
- 2 carrots, diced
- 2 leeks, sliced
- 1/4 cup (60g) celery root, diced
- 1/4 cup (60g) leek root, diced
- 6 cups (1.5 liters) beef or vegetable broth

- 1 bay leaf
- 1/4 teaspoon dried thyme
- Salt and pepper to taste

Instructions:

1. In a large pot, brown the stewing beef over medium-high heat.
2. Add the sliced sausages, chopped onion, and minced garlic. Cook for a few minutes until the onion is translucent.
3. Stir in the diced potatoes, carrots, leeks, celery root, and leek root.
4. Pour in the beef or vegetable broth and add the bay leaf and dried thyme.
5. Season with salt and pepper to taste.
6. Bring the hotpot to a boil, then reduce the heat and let it simmer for about 1.5 to 2 hours, or until the meat and vegetables are tender.
7. Remove the bay leaf before serving.

RACLETTE

Servings: 4 **Time:** 30 minutes

Ingredients:

- 1 wheel of Raclette cheese (about 2-3 pounds)
- Small, waxy potatoes, boiled and halved
- Pickles and pickled onions
- Slices of air-dried meat (e.g., prosciutto, salami)
- Slices of crusty bread

- Fresh vegetables (e.g., bell peppers, cherry tomatoes, asparagus)
- Optional: white wine

Instructions:

1. Slice the Raclette cheese into thin, even slices.
2. Arrange the boiled and halved potatoes, pickles, pickled onions, air-dried meat, slices of bread, and fresh vegetables on a platter.
3. Heat a Raclette grill or a Raclette machine.
4. Place a slice of Raclette cheese on a small pan or under the heating element of the Raclette machine.
5. Melt the cheese until it's bubbling and slightly browned.
6. Serve the melted cheese over the boiled potatoes, bread, and a selection of sides.
7. Optionally, enjoy with a glass of white wine.

SWISS MEATLOAF (HACKBRATEN)

Servings: 6 **Time:** 1 hour

Ingredients:

- 1 1/2 pounds (700g) ground beef
- 1/2 pound (225g) ground pork
- 1 cup (100g) breadcrumbs
- 1/2 cup (120ml) milk
- 1 onion, finely chopped
- 2 cloves garlic, minced
- 1/4 cup (30g) fresh parsley, chopped

- 1/4 cup (30g) Swiss cheese (Emmental or Gruyère), grated
- 2 eggs
- 1/2 teaspoon dried thyme
- Salt and pepper to taste
- 4 slices of bacon
- 1/4 cup (60ml) ketchup

Instructions:

1. Preheat your oven to 350°F (175°C).
2. In a bowl, combine the ground beef, ground pork, breadcrumbs, and milk. Let it rest for a few minutes.
3. Add the chopped onion, minced garlic, fresh parsley, grated Swiss cheese, eggs, dried thyme, salt, and pepper to the meat mixture. Mix everything thoroughly.
4. Shape the meat mixture into a loaf and place it in a baking dish.
5. Lay the bacon slices over the top of the meatloaf.
6. Brush the bacon with ketchup.
7. Bake in the preheated oven for about 45 minutes to 1 hour, or until the meatloaf is cooked through and the bacon is crispy.
8. Let it rest for a few minutes before slicing.

SWISS BRATWURST WITH RÖSTI

Servings: 4 **Time:** 45 minutes

Ingredients for Bratwurst:

- 4 Swiss Bratwurst sausages

- 1 tablespoon vegetable oil
- 1/4 cup (60ml) white wine (optional)
- Mustard for serving

Ingredients for Rösti:

- 4 large potatoes, peeled and grated
- 2 tablespoons butter
- 2 tablespoons vegetable oil
- Salt and pepper to taste

Instructions for Bratwurst:

1. Heat the vegetable oil in a skillet over medium-high heat.
2. Add the Bratwurst sausages and cook for about 15-20 minutes, turning occasionally, until they are browned and cooked through.
3. If using white wine, pour it into the skillet and let it simmer for a few minutes to create a sauce.
4. Serve the Bratwurst hot with mustard on the side.

Instructions for Rösti:

1. Place the grated potatoes in a clean kitchen towel and squeeze out any excess moisture.
2. In a large skillet, melt the butter and vegetable oil over medium heat.
3. Add the grated potatoes to the skillet, spreading them out evenly.
4. Press the potatoes down with a spatula to form a flat cake. Season with salt and pepper.
5. Cook for about 10-15 minutes, or until the bottom is golden and crispy.

SWISS COOKBOOK

6. Carefully flip the Rösti using a large plate or lid, and cook the other side until it's golden and crispy as well.
7. Once both sides are golden and the potatoes are tender, slide the Rösti onto a plate.
8. Cut into wedges and serve hot.

BERNERPLATTE (BERNESE PLATTER)

Servings: 4-6 **Time:** 2 hours

Ingredients:

- 1/2 pound (225g) smoked pork belly
- 1/2 pound (225g) smoked pork chops
- 1/2 pound (225g) smoked pork sausages
- 1/2 pound (225g) cooked ham
- 1/2 pound (225g) pork tongue or head cheese (optional)
- 4 large potatoes, peeled and boiled
- 4 large carrots, peeled and boiled
- Sauerkraut or pickled cabbage
- Mustard and horseradish for serving

Instructions:

1. In a large pot, place the smoked pork belly, smoked pork chops, smoked pork sausages, and cooked ham. Cover with water and bring to a boil.
2. Simmer for about 1 hour, or until the meats are tender.
3. Add the pork tongue or head cheese to the pot and simmer for an additional 15-20 minutes (if using).
4. Remove the meats from the pot and slice them.

5. Serve the sliced meats on a platter with boiled potatoes and boiled carrots.
6. Accompany with sauerkraut or pickled cabbage, and serve with mustard and horseradish on the side.

SWISS CHICKEN CORDON BLEU

Servings: 4 **Time:** 45 minutes

Ingredients:

- 4 boneless, skinless chicken breasts
- Salt and pepper to taste
- 4 slices Swiss cheese
- 4 slices cooked ham
- 1/2 cup (60g) all-purpose flour
- 2 large eggs
- 1 cup (100g) breadcrumbs
- 2 tablespoons vegetable oil
- Toothpicks

Instructions:

1. Preheat your oven to 350°F (175°C).
2. Place each chicken breast between two sheets of plastic wrap and gently pound them to an even thickness.
3. Season the chicken breasts with salt and pepper.
4. Place a slice of Swiss cheese and a slice of cooked ham on each chicken breast.
5. Roll up the chicken breasts, securing them with toothpicks to keep the filling inside.

6. In three separate shallow dishes, place the flour, beaten eggs, and breadcrumbs.
7. Roll each chicken roll first in the flour, then in the beaten eggs, and finally in the breadcrumbs to coat them evenly.
8. In a large skillet, heat the vegetable oil over medium-high heat.
9. Add the chicken rolls and cook for 2-3 minutes on each side until they are golden brown.
10. Transfer the browned chicken rolls to a baking dish and bake in the preheated oven for about 20-25 minutes, or until the chicken is cooked through.
11. Remove the toothpicks before serving.

SWISS BEEF STROGANOFF

Servings: 4 **Time:** 30 minutes

Ingredients:

- 1 pound (450g) beef sirloin or tenderloin, thinly sliced into strips
- 2 tablespoons butter
- 1 onion, finely chopped
- 2 cloves garlic, minced
- 1 cup (240ml) beef broth
- 1 cup (240ml) heavy cream
- 2 tablespoons all-purpose flour
- 2 tablespoons Dijon mustard
- 1 tablespoon paprika
- Salt and pepper to taste
- Fresh parsley, chopped, for garnish
- Cooked egg noodles or rice for serving

Instructions:

1. In a large skillet, heat 1 tablespoon of butter over medium-high heat.
2. Add the beef strips and cook for 2-3 minutes until they are browned. Remove the beef from the skillet and set it aside.
3. In the same skillet, add the remaining 1 tablespoon of butter and sauté the chopped onion and minced garlic until they are soft and translucent.
4. Sprinkle the flour and paprika over the onions, stirring for about a minute to create a roux.
5. Pour in the beef broth and heavy cream, whisking until the mixture thickens.
6. Return the cooked beef to the skillet and stir in the Dijon mustard.
7. Let the mixture simmer for a few minutes, or until the beef is heated through and the sauce is thick.
8. Season with salt and pepper to taste.
9. Serve your Swiss Beef Stroganoff over cooked egg noodles or rice, garnished with chopped fresh parsley.

SWISS CHICKEN FRICASSEE

Servings: 4 **Time:** 45 minutes

Ingredients:

- 4 boneless, skinless chicken breasts
- Salt and pepper to taste
- 2 tablespoons butter
- 1 onion, finely chopped

- 2 cloves garlic, minced
- 1 cup (240ml) chicken broth
- 1 cup (240ml) heavy cream
- 1/2 cup (120ml) white wine (optional)
- 2 tablespoons all-purpose flour
- 2 tablespoons fresh lemon juice
- 1/4 cup (30g) fresh parsley, chopped

Instructions:

1. Season the chicken breasts with salt and pepper.
2. In a large skillet, melt the butter over medium-high heat.
3. Add the chicken breasts and cook for about 4-5 minutes on each side until they are golden brown and cooked through. Remove the chicken from the skillet and set it aside.
4. In the same skillet, add the chopped onion and minced garlic, sautéing until they become translucent.
5. Sprinkle the flour over the onions, stirring for about a minute to create a roux.
6. Pour in the chicken broth and white wine (if using), whisking until the mixture thickens.
7. Reduce the heat to low, stir in the heavy cream, and continue to cook for a few minutes.
8. Return the cooked chicken to the skillet and simmer for a few more minutes until the chicken is heated through.
9. Stir in the fresh lemon juice and chopped fresh parsley.
10. Serve your Swiss Chicken Fricassee hot.

SWISS CHEESE AND ONION QUICHE

Servings: 6 **Time:** 1 hour

Ingredients:

- 1 pre-made pie crust (9-inch)
- 1 1/2 cups (150g) Swiss cheese, grated (Emmental or Gruyère)
- 2 onions, thinly sliced
- 2 tablespoons butter
- 4 large eggs
- 1 cup (240ml) milk
- 1/2 teaspoon salt
- 1/4 teaspoon black pepper
- 1/4 teaspoon ground nutmeg

Instructions:

1. Preheat your oven to 375°F (190°C).
2. Place the pre-made pie crust in a 9-inch pie dish and prick the bottom with a fork.
3. In a skillet, melt the butter over medium heat and sauté the thinly sliced onions until they become soft and slightly caramelized.
4. Sprinkle half of the grated Swiss cheese over the pie crust.
5. Spread the sautéed onions over the cheese in the crust.
6. Sprinkle the remaining cheese on top.
7. In a bowl, whisk together the eggs, milk, salt, black pepper, and ground nutmeg.
8. Pour the egg mixture over the cheese and onions in the pie crust.

9. Bake in the preheated oven for about 30-35 minutes, or until the quiche is set and the top is golden brown.
10. Let it cool for a few minutes before slicing.

SIDE DISHES

ALPLERMAGRONEN (SWISS ALPINE MACARONI)

Servings: 4 **Time:** 30 minutes

Ingredients:

- 8 ounces (225g) elbow macaroni or pasta of your choice
- 2 cups (480ml) milk
- 1 cup (100g) Swiss cheese, grated (Emmental or Gruyère)
- 1 cup (100g) Appenzeller cheese, grated (or more Emmental or Gruyère)
- 1 onion, finely chopped
- 2 cloves garlic, minced

- 4 slices of bacon, chopped
- 2 tablespoons butter
- Salt and pepper to taste
- Freshly grated nutmeg
- 1 apple, peeled and diced (optional)
- Fresh parsley, chopped, for garnish

Instructions:

1. Cook the elbow macaroni or pasta according to the package instructions until al dente. Drain and set aside.
2. In a large skillet, melt the butter over medium heat.
3. Add the chopped onion, minced garlic, and chopped bacon. Sauté until the onion is translucent and the bacon is crispy.
4. In a separate saucepan, heat the milk over low heat, being careful not to boil it.
5. Add the grated Swiss cheese, Appenzeller cheese, salt, and pepper to the milk. Stir until the cheese is melted and the sauce is smooth. Season with freshly grated nutmeg to taste.
6. Mix the cooked pasta with the cheese sauce and stir in the diced apple (if using).
7. Serve your Alplermagronen hot, garnished with freshly chopped parsley.

SWISS SPÄTZLI

Servings: 4 **Time:** 30 minutes

Ingredients:

- 2 cups (250g) all-purpose flour
- 3 large eggs
- 1/2 cup (120ml) milk
- Salt and pepper to taste
- 2 tablespoons butter
- Fresh parsley, chopped, for garnish

Instructions:

1. In a mixing bowl, combine the all-purpose flour, eggs, and milk. Season with salt and pepper to taste.
2. Mix the ingredients until a smooth, sticky dough forms.
3. Bring a large pot of salted water to a boil.
4. To make the Spätzli, you have a few options:
    - You can use a Spätzli maker if you have one, which will help you form the traditional shape. Simply press the dough through the holes into the boiling water.
    - Alternatively, you can use a colander or a slotted spoon to drop small, irregular pieces of dough into the water.
5. Cook the Spätzli for about 2-3 minutes or until they rise to the surface.
6. Use a slotted spoon to remove the cooked Spätzli and place them in a bowl of cold water to cool.
7. In a skillet, melt the butter over medium heat.
8. Drain the Spätzli and sauté them in the melted butter until they become lightly golden.
9. Garnish with chopped fresh parsley and serve hot.

SWISS RED CABBAGE

Servings: 4 **Time:** 45 minutes

Ingredients:

- 1 small head of red cabbage, thinly sliced
- 1 onion, finely chopped
- 2 apples, peeled, cored, and sliced
- 2 tablespoons butter
- 2 tablespoons red wine vinegar
- 2 tablespoons sugar
- 1/2 cup (120ml) vegetable or beef broth
- Salt and pepper to taste

Instructions:

1. In a large skillet, melt the butter over medium heat.
2. Add the finely chopped onion and sauté until it becomes translucent.
3. Stir in the thinly sliced red cabbage and apple slices.
4. Add the red wine vinegar and sugar, then pour in the vegetable or beef broth.
5. Season with salt and pepper to taste.
6. Cover the skillet and let the red cabbage simmer for about 30-35 minutes, or until it's tender and the liquid has reduced.
7. Adjust the seasoning if needed.
8. Serve your Swiss Red Cabbage hot as a flavorful side dish.

SWISS CREAMED SPINACH

Servings: 4 **Time:** 20 minutes

Ingredients:

- 1 pound (450g) fresh spinach, washed and trimmed
- 2 tablespoons butter
- 2 tablespoons all-purpose flour
- 1 cup (240ml) milk
- 1/4 cup (30g) Swiss cheese, grated (Emmental or Gruyère)
- Salt and pepper to taste
- Ground nutmeg to taste

Instructions:

1. In a large pot, bring a small amount of water to a boil. Add the fresh spinach and blanch for about 2-3 minutes until it wilts. Drain and set aside.
2. In a saucepan, melt the butter over medium heat.
3. Stir in the all-purpose flour and cook for a minute or until it turns slightly golden.
4. Gradually whisk in the milk and continue to cook, stirring until the mixture thickens.
5. Add the grated Swiss cheese, salt, pepper, and a sprinkle of ground nutmeg. Stir until the cheese is melted and the sauce is smooth.
6. Chop the blanched spinach and stir it into the cheese sauce.
7. Cook for an additional 2-3 minutes, allowing the spinach to heat through.
8. Serve your Swiss Creamed Spinach hot as a creamy and delightful side dish.

SWISS GLACE DE VIANDE (GRAVY)

Servings: Approximately 1 cup **Time:** 30 minutes

Ingredients:

- 1 cup (240ml) beef or veal stock
- 2 tablespoons butter
- 2 tablespoons all-purpose flour
- Salt and pepper to taste

Instructions:

1. In a saucepan, melt the butter over medium heat.
2. Sprinkle in the all-purpose flour and cook, stirring continuously, until it turns a light golden brown and forms a smooth roux.
3. Gradually whisk in the beef or veal stock to the roux, ensuring there are no lumps.
4. Simmer the mixture for about 15-20 minutes, allowing it to reduce and thicken to your desired consistency.
5. Season with salt and pepper to taste.
6. Strain the gravy through a fine sieve to remove any remaining lumps.
7. Serve your Swiss Glace de Viande hot as a rich sauce for various meat dishes.

SWISS VEGETABLE GRATIN

Servings: 4 **Time:** 45 minutes

Ingredients:

- 2 cups (200g) mixed vegetables (e.g., broccoli, cauliflower, carrots), steamed and chopped

- 2 tablespoons butter
- 2 tablespoons all-purpose flour
- 1 cup (240ml) milk
- 1/2 cup (50g) Swiss cheese, grated (Emmental or Gruyère)
- Salt and pepper to taste
- 1/4 cup (25g) breadcrumbs
- Fresh parsley, chopped, for garnish (optional)

Instructions:

1. Preheat your oven to 350°F (175°C).
2. In a saucepan, melt the butter over medium heat.
3. Stir in the all-purpose flour and cook for a minute to form a roux.
4. Gradually whisk in the milk, ensuring there are no lumps. Continue to cook and stir until the mixture thickens.
5. Add the grated Swiss cheese, salt, and pepper. Stir until the cheese is melted and the sauce is smooth.
6. Place the steamed and chopped mixed vegetables in a baking dish.
7. Pour the cheese sauce over the vegetables, ensuring they are evenly coated.
8. Sprinkle the breadcrumbs on top.
9. Bake in the preheated oven for about 20-25 minutes, or until the gratin is golden and bubbling.
10. If desired, garnish with chopped fresh parsley before serving.

SWISS SWEET POTATO GRATIN

Servings: 4 **Time:** 1 hour

Ingredients:

- 2 large sweet potatoes, peeled and thinly sliced
- 1 cup (240ml) heavy cream
- 1/2 cup (50g) Swiss cheese, grated (Emmental or Gruyère)
- 2 cloves garlic, minced
- 1 teaspoon fresh rosemary, chopped
- Salt and pepper to taste
- 1/4 cup (25g) breadcrumbs
- 2 tablespoons butter
- Fresh parsley, chopped, for garnish (optional)

Instructions:

1. Preheat your oven to 350°F (175°C).
2. In a bowl, mix the heavy cream, grated Swiss cheese, minced garlic, chopped fresh rosemary, salt, and pepper.
3. Layer half of the sliced sweet potatoes in a baking dish.
4. Pour half of the cream mixture over the sweet potatoes.
5. Repeat with the remaining sweet potatoes and cream mixture.
6. In a separate bowl, combine the breadcrumbs and melted butter.
7. Sprinkle the breadcrumb mixture on top of the sweet potatoes.
8. Cover the baking dish with aluminum foil and bake for about 45 minutes.

9. Remove the foil and bake for an additional 10-15 minutes, or until the sweet potatoes are tender and the gratin is golden and bubbly.
10. If desired, garnish with chopped fresh parsley before serving.

BREADS AND PASTRIES

SWISS ZOPF (BRAIDED BREAD)

Servings: 1 loaf **Time:** 2 hours

Ingredients:

- 4 cups (500g) all-purpose flour
- 1 1/2 teaspoons salt
- 1/4 cup (60g) granulated sugar
- 2 1/4 teaspoons (7g) active dry yeast
- 1 cup (240ml) warm milk
- 4 tablespoons (60g) unsalted butter, softened
- 1 egg, beaten (for egg wash)

Instructions:

1. In a small bowl, combine the warm milk and active dry yeast. Let it sit for about 5 minutes, or until it becomes foamy.
2. In a large mixing bowl, whisk together the all-purpose flour, salt, and sugar.
3. Make a well in the center of the dry ingredients and pour in the yeast mixture.
4. Add the softened butter to the bowl.
5. Knead the mixture until you have a smooth, elastic dough, about 10-15 minutes.
6. Shape the dough into a ball, cover the bowl with a kitchen towel, and let it rise in a warm place for about 1 hour, or until it has doubled in size.
7. Preheat your oven to 350°F (175°C).
8. Punch down the risen dough and divide it into 3 equal portions.
9. Roll each portion into a long rope, approximately 20-24 inches (50-60 cm) in length.
10. Braid the ropes together to form a loaf, tucking the ends under.
11. Place the braided loaf on a baking sheet lined with parchment paper.
12. Brush the loaf with the beaten egg to give it a glossy finish.
13. Bake in the preheated oven for about 25-30 minutes, or until the Zopf is golden brown and sounds hollow when tapped on the bottom.
14. Let it cool on a wire rack before slicing and serving.

SWISS RÜEBLITORTE (CARROT CAKE)

Servings: 8-10 **Time:** 1 hour

Ingredients:

- 2 cups (250g) carrots, finely grated
- 1 cup (200g) granulated sugar
- 4 large eggs
- 1 teaspoon vanilla extract
- 1/2 cup (120ml) vegetable oil
- 1 cup (125g) all-purpose flour
- 1 1/2 teaspoons baking powder
- 1/2 teaspoon ground cinnamon
- 1/2 cup (50g) ground almonds
- 1/2 cup (50g) grated Swiss chocolate (or dark chocolate)
- Powdered sugar for dusting (optional)

Instructions:

1. Preheat your oven to 350°F (175°C) and grease a 9-inch (23cm) round cake pan.
2. In a large mixing bowl, combine the finely grated carrots and granulated sugar. Let it sit for about 10 minutes to allow the carrots to release some moisture.
3. After 10 minutes, beat in the eggs, one at a time, and add the vanilla extract and vegetable oil.
4. In a separate bowl, whisk together the all-purpose flour, baking powder, ground cinnamon, and ground almonds.
5. Gradually add the dry ingredients to the carrot mixture, stirring until well combined.
6. Stir in the grated Swiss chocolate (or dark chocolate).
7. Pour the batter into the prepared cake pan.

8. Bake in the preheated oven for about 35-40 minutes, or until a toothpick inserted into the center comes out clean.
9. Let the Rüeblitorte cool in the pan for a few minutes, then transfer it to a wire rack to cool completely.
10. Optionally, dust the cake with powdered sugar before serving.

NUSSTORTE (SWISS NUT TART)

Servings: 8-10 **Time:** 1 hour

Ingredients for the Crust:

- 1 1/2 cups (190g) all-purpose flour
- 1/2 cup (60g) ground walnuts
- 1/2 cup (60g) powdered sugar
- 1/2 cup (120g) unsalted butter, cold and cubed
- 1 egg

Ingredients for the Filling:

- 1 1/2 cups (150g) ground walnuts
- 1/2 cup (60g) powdered sugar
- 1/2 cup (120ml) heavy cream
- 2 tablespoons honey
- 1/4 cup (60g) unsalted butter
- 1 teaspoon vanilla extract
- 1/4 teaspoon ground cinnamon

Instructions:

For the Crust:

1. In a food processor, combine the all-purpose flour, ground walnuts, and powdered sugar.
2. Add the cold, cubed unsalted butter and pulse until the mixture resembles coarse crumbs.
3. Add the egg and pulse until the dough comes together.
4. Remove the dough from the food processor and shape it into a disk. Wrap it in plastic wrap and refrigerate for 30 minutes.

For the Filling:

1. In a saucepan, combine the ground walnuts, powdered sugar, heavy cream, honey, unsalted butter, vanilla extract, and ground cinnamon.
2. Cook over medium heat, stirring continuously, until the mixture thickens and comes away from the sides of the pan. This should take about 10-15 minutes.
3. Remove the filling from the heat and let it cool.

Assembly:

1. Preheat your oven to 350°F (175°C).
2. Roll out the chilled dough on a floured surface to fit a 9-inch (23cm) tart pan.
3. Press the dough into the tart pan and trim any excess.
4. Prick the bottom of the crust with a fork and bake it in the preheated oven for about 10-12 minutes, or until it's lightly golden.
5. Remove the pre-baked crust from the oven and let it cool slightly.
6. Pour the cooled nut filling into the crust and spread it evenly.

7. Bake the tart for an additional 25-30 minutes, or until the filling is set and the top is golden.
8. Let the Nusstorte cool before slicing and serving.

SWISS BIBERLI (HONEY-GLAZED COOKIES)

Servings: 20 cookies **Time:** 1 hour

Ingredients:

For the Dough:

- 2 cups (250g) all-purpose flour
- 1/2 teaspoon ground cinnamon
- 1/4 teaspoon ground cloves
- 1/4 teaspoon ground nutmeg
- 1/2 cup (100g) granulated sugar
- 1/2 cup (120g) unsalted butter, softened
- 1/4 cup (60ml) honey
- 1 egg
- 1/2 cup (60g) ground almonds
- 1/4 cup (60ml) Kirsch (cherry brandy) or water

For the Glaze:

- 1 cup (120g) powdered sugar
- 2-3 tablespoons lemon juice
- Colored sprinkles (optional)

Instructions:

For the Dough:

1. In a mixing bowl, combine the all-purpose flour, ground cinnamon, ground cloves, and ground nutmeg.
2. In a separate bowl, beat together the granulated sugar, softened unsalted butter, honey, and egg until well combined.
3. Gradually add the dry ingredients to the wet ingredients, mixing until a dough forms.
4. Stir in the ground almonds and Kirsch (or water) to create a smooth dough.
5. Wrap the dough in plastic wrap and refrigerate it for 30 minutes.

For the Glaze:

1. In a small bowl, whisk together the powdered sugar and lemon juice until you achieve a thick but pourable glaze. Adjust the consistency with more sugar or lemon juice as needed.

Assembly:

1. Preheat your oven to 350°F (175°C) and line a baking sheet with parchment paper.
2. Roll out the chilled dough on a floured surface to about 1/4-inch (0.6cm) thickness.
3. Use cookie cutters to cut out your desired shapes, and place them on the prepared baking sheet.
4. Bake in the preheated oven for about 12-15 minutes, or until the cookies are lightly golden.
5. Remove the cookies from the oven and let them cool on a wire rack.

6. Once the cookies are cool, drizzle them with the lemon glaze and add colored sprinkles if desired.
7. Let the glaze set before serving.

BASLER LÄCKERLI (SWISS GINGERBREAD)

Servings: 24 pieces **Time:** 1 hour

Ingredients:

For the Dough:

- 2 cups (250g) all-purpose flour
- 1/2 teaspoon ground cinnamon
- 1/4 teaspoon ground cloves
- 1/4 teaspoon ground nutmeg
- 1 cup (200g) granulated sugar
- 1/3 cup (80ml) honey
- 2 tablespoons kirsch (cherry brandy) or water
- Zest of 1 lemon
- 1 1/2 cups (180g) mixed candied peel, chopped
- 1/2 cup (60g) ground almonds
- 1/4 cup (60g) unsalted butter, melted

For the Glaze:

- 1 cup (120g) powdered sugar
- 2-3 tablespoons lemon juice

Instructions:

For the Dough:

1. In a mixing bowl, combine the all-purpose flour, ground cinnamon, ground cloves, and ground nutmeg.
2. In a separate saucepan, heat the granulated sugar, honey, kirsch (or water), and lemon zest over low heat, stirring until the sugar dissolves.
3. Stir in the chopped candied peel and ground almonds.
4. Pour the sugar mixture over the dry ingredients and stir to form a thick, sticky dough.
5. Add the melted unsalted butter and mix until well combined.
6. Preheat your oven to 350°F (175°C) and line a baking sheet with parchment paper.

Assembly:

1. Roll out the dough on a floured surface to about 1/4-inch (0.6cm) thickness.
2. Cut the dough into small rectangular pieces or your desired shapes and place them on the prepared baking sheet.
3. Bake in the preheated oven for about 20-25 minutes, or until the cookies are lightly golden.
4. Remove the cookies from the oven and let them cool on a wire rack.
5. In a small bowl, whisk together the powdered sugar and lemon juice to create a glaze.
6. Drizzle the lemon glaze over the cooled cookies.
7. Let the glaze set before serving.

ZUGER KIRSCHTORTE (CHERRY CAKE)

Servings: 10-12 **Time:** 2 hours

Ingredients:

For the Cake Layers:

- 1 cup (120g) ground almonds
- 1/2 cup (60g) all-purpose flour
- 1/2 cup (120g) granulated sugar
- 4 large eggs, separated
- 1/4 cup (60ml) Kirsch (cherry brandy)

For the Cherry Filling:

- 2 cups (300g) fresh or canned pitted cherries
- 1/4 cup (60ml) Kirsch (cherry brandy)
- 1/2 cup (100g) granulated sugar

For the Whipped Cream Topping:

- 2 cups (480ml) heavy cream
- 1/4 cup (30g) powdered sugar
- 1 teaspoon vanilla extract

Instructions:

For the Cake Layers:

1. Preheat your oven to 350°F (175°C). Grease and line the bottom of two 8-inch (20cm) round cake pans with parchment paper.
2. In a bowl, combine the ground almonds, all-purpose flour, and granulated sugar.

3. In a separate bowl, beat the egg yolks until they are pale and creamy.
4. Stir the beaten egg yolks into the dry mixture.
5. In another clean bowl, whip the egg whites until stiff peaks form.
6. Gently fold the whipped egg whites into the batter.
7. Stir in the Kirsch (cherry brandy).
8. Divide the batter between the two prepared cake pans.
9. Bake in the preheated oven for about 20-25 minutes or until a toothpick inserted into the center comes out clean.
10. Allow the cake layers to cool in the pans for a few minutes, then transfer them to a wire rack to cool completely.

For the Cherry Filling:

1. In a saucepan, combine the pitted cherries, Kirsch (cherry brandy), and granulated sugar.
2. Cook over low heat, stirring, until the cherries are soft and the mixture thickens. This should take about 10-15 minutes.
3. Let the cherry filling cool.

For the Whipped Cream Topping:

1. In a mixing bowl, whip the heavy cream, powdered sugar, and vanilla extract until stiff peaks form.

Assembly:

1. Place one cake layer on a serving plate.
2. Spread half of the cherry filling over the cake layer.

3. Add a layer of whipped cream on top of the cherry filling.
4. Place the second cake layer on top.
5. Spread the remaining cherry filling over the second cake layer.
6. Cover the entire cake with the remaining whipped cream.
7. You can garnish the Zuger Kirschtorte with additional cherries, chocolate shavings, or almonds if desired.

SWISS BUTTERZOPF

Servings: 1 loaf **Time:** 2 hours

Ingredients:

For the Dough:

- 4 cups (500g) all-purpose flour
- 1 1/2 teaspoons salt
- 1/4 cup (50g) granulated sugar
- 1 1/2 teaspoons active dry yeast
- 1/2 cup (120ml) whole milk, lukewarm
- 1/2 cup (120ml) water, lukewarm
- 4 tablespoons (60g) unsalted butter, softened
- 1 egg, beaten (for egg wash)

Instructions:

For the Dough:

1. In a small bowl, combine the lukewarm whole milk and lukewarm water. Sprinkle the active dry yeast over the liquid, and let it sit for about 5-10 minutes, or until it becomes frothy.
2. In a large mixing bowl, whisk together the all-purpose flour, salt, and granulated sugar.
3. Make a well in the center of the dry ingredients and pour in the yeast mixture.
4. Add the softened unsalted butter to the bowl.
5. Knead the mixture until you have a smooth, elastic dough, about 10-15 minutes.
6. Shape the dough into a ball, cover the bowl with a kitchen towel, and let it rise in a warm place for about 1 hour, or until it has doubled in size.
7. Preheat your oven to 350°F (175°C).
8. Punch down the risen dough and divide it into three equal portions.
9. Roll each portion into a long rope, approximately 20-24 inches (50-60 cm) in length.
10. Braid the ropes together to form a loaf, tucking the ends under.
11. Place the braided loaf on a baking sheet lined with parchment paper.
12. Brush the loaf with the beaten egg to give it a glossy finish.
13. Bake in the preheated oven for about 25-30 minutes, or until the Butterzopf is golden brown and sounds hollow when tapped on the bottom.
14. Let it cool on a wire rack before slicing and serving.

SWISS CHOCOLATE MOUSSE CAKE

Servings: 8-10 **Time:** 2 hours (plus chilling time)

Ingredients:

For the Chocolate Cake:

- 1 1/2 cups (190g) all-purpose flour
- 1 1/2 cups (300g) granulated sugar
- 3/4 cup (75g) unsweetened cocoa powder
- 1 1/2 teaspoons baking powder
- 1 1/2 teaspoons baking soda
- 1 teaspoon salt
- 2 large eggs
- 1 cup (240ml) buttermilk
- 1/2 cup (120ml) vegetable oil
- 2 teaspoons pure vanilla extract
- 1 cup (240ml) boiling water

For the Chocolate Mousse:

- 8 ounces (225g) semisweet chocolate, chopped
- 1 1/2 cups (360ml) heavy cream
- 1/4 cup (30g) powdered sugar
- 2 teaspoons pure vanilla extract

For the Chocolate Ganache:

- 4 ounces (115g) semisweet chocolate, chopped
- 1/2 cup (120ml) heavy cream
- 1 tablespoon unsalted butter

Instructions:

For the Chocolate Cake:

1. Preheat your oven to 350°F (175°C). Grease and line the bottom of a 9-inch (23cm) round cake pan with parchment paper.
2. In a large mixing bowl, whisk together the all-purpose flour, granulated sugar, cocoa powder, baking powder, baking soda, and salt.
3. Add the eggs, buttermilk, vegetable oil, and vanilla extract to the dry ingredients and mix until well combined.
4. Stir in the boiling water until the batter is smooth. The batter will be thin, but that's okay.
5. Pour the batter into the prepared cake pan.
6. Bake in the preheated oven for about 30-35 minutes, or until a toothpick inserted into the center comes out clean.
7. Allow the cake to cool in the pan for 10 minutes before transferring it to a wire rack to cool completely.

For the Chocolate Mousse:

1. Place the chopped semisweet chocolate in a heatproof bowl.
2. In a saucepan, heat 1/2 cup of heavy cream until it begins to simmer. Do not boil.
3. Pour the hot cream over the chocolate and let it sit for a minute.
4. Stir the mixture until the chocolate is completely melted and the mixture is smooth.
5. Allow the chocolate mixture to cool to room temperature.

6. In a separate bowl, whip the remaining 1 cup of heavy cream, powdered sugar, and vanilla extract until stiff peaks form.
7. Gently fold the whipped cream into the cooled chocolate mixture to create the mousse.

For the Chocolate Ganache:

1. Place the chopped semisweet chocolate and butter in a heatproof bowl.
2. In a saucepan, heat the 1/2 cup of heavy cream until it begins to simmer. Do not boil.
3. Pour the hot cream over the chocolate and butter and let it sit for a minute.
4. Stir the mixture until the chocolate and butter are completely melted and the ganache is smooth.

Assembly:

1. Once the cake has cooled, use a serrated knife to level the top if necessary.
2. Place the cake on a serving platter.
3. Spread a layer of chocolate mousse on top of the cake.
4. Gently place a second cake layer on top of the mousse and repeat the process until all layers are used.
5. Pour the chocolate ganache over the top of the cake, allowing it to drip down the sides.
6. Refrigerate the cake for at least 4 hours, or until the mousse and ganache are set.
7. Before serving, you can garnish with chocolate shavings or berries if desired.

CHEESE DISHES

CHEESE SLICES (KÄSESCHNITTEN)

Servings: 4 **Time:** 15 minutes

Ingredients:

For the Cheese Slices:

- 4 slices of Swiss bread (e.g., rustic country bread)
- 8 slices of Swiss cheese (Emmental or Gruyère)
- 4 eggs
- 1/4 cup (60ml) milk
- Salt and pepper to taste
- 2 tablespoons butter

For Garnish (optional):

- Chopped fresh parsley or chives

Instructions:

1. In a bowl, whisk together the eggs, milk, salt, and pepper until well combined.
2. Place a slice of Swiss cheese on each slice of bread.
3. In a large skillet, melt the butter over medium heat.
4. Dip each cheese-topped bread slice into the egg mixture, ensuring they are evenly coated on both sides.
5. Place the coated bread slices in the skillet and cook until golden brown on one side, about 2-3 minutes.
6. Carefully flip the slices and cook the other side until it's also golden brown and the cheese is melted.
7. Once the cheese slices are cooked, transfer them to a serving plate.
8. If desired, garnish with chopped fresh parsley or chives.

SWISS CHEESE AND HERB PANCAKES

Servings: 4 **Time:** 20 minutes

Ingredients:

For the Pancakes:

- 1 cup (125g) all-purpose flour
- 1 teaspoon baking powder
- 1/2 teaspoon salt
- 1/4 teaspoon black pepper
- 1 cup (240ml) milk

- 1 egg
- 1/2 cup (50g) grated Swiss cheese (Emmental or Gruyère)
- 2 tablespoons fresh herbs (e.g., chives, parsley, or thyme), chopped
- 2 tablespoons unsalted butter, melted

For the Topping:

- Additional grated Swiss cheese
- Fresh herbs for garnish (optional)

Instructions:

1. In a mixing bowl, whisk together the all-purpose flour, baking powder, salt, and black pepper.
2. In a separate bowl, beat the egg and then stir in the milk.
3. Pour the egg and milk mixture into the dry ingredients and mix until well combined.
4. Stir in the grated Swiss cheese, chopped fresh herbs, and melted butter.
5. Preheat a non-stick skillet or griddle over medium heat and lightly grease it with butter or cooking spray.
6. Pour a ladle of pancake batter onto the skillet to form each pancake. You can adjust the size to your preference.
7. Cook until the edges of the pancake appear set and there are bubbles on the surface, about 2-3 minutes.
8. Sprinkle additional grated Swiss cheese on top of each pancake.

9. Flip the pancakes and cook for an additional 2-3 minutes, or until they are golden and the cheese is melted.
10. Remove the pancakes from the skillet and garnish with fresh herbs if desired.

CHEESE AND POTATO DUMPLINGS

Servings: 4 **Time:** 45 minutes

Ingredients:

For the Dumplings:

- 2 cups (400g) potatoes, peeled and diced
- 1 cup (100g) Swiss cheese (Emmental or Gruyère), grated
- 1/4 cup (30g) all-purpose flour
- 1 egg, beaten
- Salt and pepper to taste
- 2 tablespoons butter

For the Sauce:

- 1/2 cup (120ml) heavy cream
- 1/2 cup (120ml) vegetable or chicken broth
- 2 tablespoons butter
- 1/4 cup (30g) Swiss cheese, grated
- Salt and pepper to taste
- Chopped fresh chives for garnish (optional)

Instructions:

For the Dumplings:

1. Place the peeled and diced potatoes in a pot of salted water and bring it to a boil. Cook until the potatoes are tender, about 15-20 minutes.
2. Drain the cooked potatoes and transfer them to a mixing bowl.
3. Mash the potatoes until they are smooth.
4. Add the grated Swiss cheese, all-purpose flour, beaten egg, salt, and pepper to the mashed potatoes. Mix until the ingredients are well combined.
5. With floured hands, shape the mixture into small dumplings, about the size of a golf ball.

For the Sauce:

1. In a saucepan, heat the heavy cream and vegetable or chicken broth over low heat. Do not boil.
2. Stir in the butter and grated Swiss cheese until the sauce is smooth and the cheese is melted.
3. Season the sauce with salt and pepper to taste.

Assembly:

1. In a large skillet, melt the 2 tablespoons of butter over medium heat.
2. Add the potato dumplings to the skillet and cook until they are golden brown on all sides, about 5-7 minutes.
3. Pour the cheese sauce over the dumplings and gently stir to coat them.

4. Allow the dumplings to simmer in the sauce for a few minutes, until they are heated through and the sauce thickens.
5. If desired, garnish with chopped fresh chives before serving.

SWISS CHEESE GNOCCHI

Servings: 4 **Time:** 1 hour

Ingredients:

For the Gnocchi:

- 2 pounds (900g) potatoes, unpeeled
- 1 1/2 cups (180g) all-purpose flour, plus more for dusting
- 1 cup (100g) Swiss cheese (Emmental or Gruyère), grated
- 1 egg, beaten
- Salt and pepper to taste

For the Sauce:

- 2 tablespoons unsalted butter
- 2 tablespoons all-purpose flour
- 1 1/2 cups (360ml) milk
- 1 cup (100g) Swiss cheese, grated
- Salt and pepper to taste
- Grated nutmeg for seasoning (optional)

Instructions:

For the Gnocchi:

1. In a large pot, boil the unpeeled potatoes until they are tender, about 20-25 minutes.
2. Drain and peel the hot potatoes while they are still warm. Use a potato ricer or masher to mash the potatoes until smooth.
3. In a mixing bowl, combine the mashed potatoes, all-purpose flour, grated Swiss cheese, beaten egg, salt, and pepper.
4. Knead the mixture into a smooth dough, adding more flour if needed to prevent sticking.
5. On a floured surface, roll the dough into long ropes, about 1-inch (2.5cm) in diameter.
6. Cut the ropes into bite-sized pieces and use the tines of a fork to create ridges on each gnocchi.

For the Sauce:

1. In a saucepan, melt the butter over medium heat.
2. Stir in the all-purpose flour and cook for a minute or two until it forms a smooth paste (roux).
3. Gradually pour in the milk while whisking constantly to prevent lumps.
4. Cook the sauce, stirring, until it thickens and begins to simmer.
5. Remove the saucepan from the heat and stir in the grated Swiss cheese until it's fully melted. Season with salt, pepper, and a touch of grated nutmeg if desired.

Assembly:

1. Bring a large pot of salted water to a boil.
2. Carefully drop the gnocchi into the boiling water and cook until they float to the surface, which should take about 2-3 minutes.
3. Remove the gnocchi with a slotted spoon and place them on serving plates.
4. Pour the Swiss cheese sauce over the cooked gnocchi.
5. Optionally, garnish with more grated Swiss cheese and a pinch of nutmeg.

SWISS CHEESE AND ONION SOUP

Servings: 4 **Time:** 1 hour

Ingredients:

For the Soup:

- 4 large onions, thinly sliced
- 3 tablespoons unsalted butter
- 1 tablespoon olive oil
- 1 tablespoon all-purpose flour
- 4 cups (960ml) beef or vegetable broth
- 1 bay leaf
- 1 teaspoon fresh thyme leaves (or 1/2 teaspoon dried thyme)
- Salt and black pepper to taste

For the Topping:

- 4 slices of Swiss cheese (Emmental or Gruyère)
- 4 slices of baguette or French bread
- Butter for spreading on the bread (optional)

Instructions:

For the Soup:

1. In a large pot, heat the butter and olive oil over medium-low heat.
2. Add the thinly sliced onions and cook, stirring occasionally, until they become soft and golden brown, about 30-40 minutes.
3. Sprinkle the all-purpose flour over the caramelized onions and cook for an additional 2-3 minutes, stirring to incorporate the flour.
4. Pour in the beef or vegetable broth, add the bay leaf, thyme, and season with salt and black pepper.
5. Bring the soup to a gentle simmer and let it cook for about 15-20 minutes to allow the flavors to meld.
6. Remove the bay leaf.

For the Topping:

1. Preheat your broiler.
2. If desired, spread a bit of butter on the slices of baguette.
3. Place a slice of Swiss cheese on each slice of bread.
4. Broil the cheese-topped bread slices until they are bubbly and golden brown, about 2-3 minutes. Keep a close eye to prevent burning.

Assembly:

1. Ladle the Swiss Cheese and Onion Soup into individual serving bowls.
2. Place a slice of the cheesy bread on top of each bowl of soup.

3. Serve the soup hot, and enjoy the gooey, cheesy goodness!

SWISS CHEESE STUFFED MUSHROOMS

Servings: 4 **Time:** 30 minutes

Ingredients:

For the Stuffed Mushrooms:

- 16 large mushrooms, cleaned and stems removed
- 1/2 cup (50g) Swiss cheese (Emmental or Gruyère), grated
- 1/4 cup (25g) breadcrumbs
- 2 tablespoons fresh parsley, finely chopped
- 1 garlic clove, minced
- 2 tablespoons olive oil
- Salt and black pepper to taste

Instructions:

1. Preheat your oven to 350°F (175°C).

For the Stuffed Mushrooms:

1. In a bowl, combine the Swiss cheese, breadcrumbs, chopped fresh parsley, and minced garlic. Mix well.
2. Season the mixture with salt and black pepper to taste.
3. Stuff each mushroom cap with the cheese and breadcrumb mixture, pressing it down gently.
4. Place the stuffed mushrooms on a baking sheet.

5. Drizzle olive oil over the stuffed mushrooms.
6. Bake in the preheated oven for about 15-20 minutes, or until the mushrooms are tender and the cheese is melted and golden.
7. Serve the Swiss Cheese Stuffed Mushrooms hot as a delightful appetizer or side dish.

CHEESE AND SPINACH STUFFED CHICKEN

Servings: 4 **Time:** 45 minutes

Ingredients:

For the Stuffed Chicken:

- 4 boneless, skinless chicken breasts
- 1 cup (100g) Swiss cheese (Emmental or Gruyère), shredded
- 1 cup (100g) fresh spinach, chopped
- 2 cloves garlic, minced
- 1/4 cup (60ml) heavy cream
- Salt and black pepper to taste
- 2 tablespoons olive oil

For the Coating:

- 1 cup (125g) all-purpose flour
- 2 large eggs, beaten
- 1 cup (100g) breadcrumbs
- Salt and black pepper to taste

Instructions:

For the Stuffed Chicken:

1. Preheat your oven to 375°F (190°C).
2. Make a horizontal cut in each chicken breast to create a pocket for the stuffing. Be careful not to cut all the way through.
3. In a mixing bowl, combine the shredded Swiss cheese, chopped fresh spinach, minced garlic, heavy cream, salt, and black pepper. Mix until well combined.
4. Carefully stuff each chicken breast with the cheese and spinach mixture.
5. Secure the openings with toothpicks to keep the filling in place.
6. Season the outside of the chicken breasts with a bit of salt and black pepper.

For the Coating:

1. Place the all-purpose flour, beaten eggs, and breadcrumbs in three separate shallow dishes.
2. Dredge each stuffed chicken breast in the flour, ensuring it's well-coated.
3. Dip the floured chicken into the beaten eggs, allowing any excess to drip off.
4. Roll the chicken in the breadcrumbs, pressing them onto the surface to adhere.

Cooking the Chicken:

1. Heat the olive oil in an ovenproof skillet over medium-high heat.

2. Place the coated chicken breasts in the skillet and cook for about 2-3 minutes on each side, or until they are golden brown.
3. Transfer the skillet to the preheated oven and bake for an additional 20-25 minutes, or until the chicken is cooked through and the cheese is melted and bubbly.
4. If you don't have an ovenproof skillet, you can transfer the browned chicken to a baking dish before baking.

Final Steps:

1. Remove the toothpicks from the chicken.
2. Serve the Cheese and Spinach Stuffed Chicken hot, garnished with additional fresh spinach or herbs if desired.

VEGETARIAN DISHES

SWISS CHEESE AND MUSHROOM RISOTTO

Servings: 4 **Time:** 30 minutes

Ingredients:

- 1 1/2 cups (300g) Arborio rice
- 4 cups (960ml) vegetable broth
- 1 cup (240ml) dry white wine
- 1 cup (100g) Swiss cheese (Emmental or Gruyère), grated
- 8 ounces (225g) mushrooms (e.g., cremini or white), sliced
- 1 small onion, finely chopped
- 2 cloves garlic, minced

- 2 tablespoons butter
- 2 tablespoons olive oil
- 2 tablespoons fresh parsley, chopped
- Salt and black pepper to taste
- Grated Parmesan cheese for garnish (optional)

Instructions:

1. In a saucepan, heat the vegetable broth and keep it warm over low heat.
2. In a large skillet or saucepan, heat the olive oil and 1 tablespoon of butter over medium heat.
3. Add the chopped onion and sauté for 2-3 minutes until it becomes translucent.
4. Stir in the minced garlic and cook for an additional 30 seconds until fragrant.
5. Add the Arborio rice to the skillet and cook, stirring, for about 2 minutes until the rice grains become slightly translucent.
6. Pour in the white wine and cook, stirring, until the wine is mostly absorbed by the rice.
7. Begin adding the warm vegetable broth, one ladleful at a time, to the rice. Stir constantly and allow the liquid to be absorbed before adding more. Continue this process until the rice is al dente, which should take about 18-20 minutes.
8. While cooking the risotto, in a separate skillet, heat the remaining 1 tablespoon of butter. Sauté the sliced mushrooms until they are tender and browned. Season with salt and black pepper to taste.
9. Once the risotto is cooked to your liking, stir in the grated Swiss cheese until it's fully melted and creamy.

10. Add the sautéed mushrooms to the risotto and mix them in.
11. Stir in the fresh parsley.
12. Taste the risotto and adjust the seasoning with salt and black pepper if necessary.
13. Serve the Swiss Cheese and Mushroom Risotto hot, garnished with grated Parmesan cheese if desired.

SWISS CHEESE AND SPINACH QUICHE

Servings: 6-8 **Time:** 1 hour

Ingredients:

For the Quiche Crust:

- 1 1/4 cups (155g) all-purpose flour
- 1/2 teaspoon salt
- 1/2 cup (115g) unsalted butter, cold and cubed
- 3-4 tablespoons ice-cold water

For the Quiche Filling:

- 1 cup (100g) Swiss cheese (Emmental or Gruyère), grated
- 1 cup (100g) fresh spinach, chopped
- 4 large eggs
- 1 cup (240ml) heavy cream
- 1/2 teaspoon salt
- 1/4 teaspoon black pepper
- A pinch of nutmeg (optional)

Instructions:

For the Quiche Crust:

1. In a food processor, combine the all-purpose flour and salt.
2. Add the cold, cubed unsalted butter and pulse until the mixture resembles coarse crumbs.
3. Gradually add the ice-cold water and pulse until the dough starts to come together.
4. Turn the dough out onto a floured surface and shape it into a disc.
5. Wrap the dough in plastic wrap and refrigerate for at least 30 minutes.

For the Quiche Filling:

1. Preheat your oven to 375°F (190°C).
2. Roll out the chilled quiche crust on a floured surface and line a 9-inch (23cm) pie dish or quiche pan with the crust.
3. Prick the bottom of the crust with a fork, and then line it with parchment paper and fill it with pie weights or dried beans. Bake the crust for about 15 minutes.
4. Remove the parchment paper and weights, and bake for an additional 5 minutes, or until the crust is lightly golden. Remove it from the oven and let it cool slightly.
5. In a mixing bowl, whisk together the eggs, heavy cream, salt, black pepper, and nutmeg (if using).
6. Sprinkle the grated Swiss cheese evenly over the pre-baked crust.
7. Add the chopped fresh spinach on top of the cheese.
8. Pour the egg and cream mixture over the cheese and spinach.

9. Place the quiche in the preheated oven and bake for about 30-35 minutes, or until the quiche is set and the top is golden brown.
10. Let the Swiss Cheese and Spinach Quiche cool for a few minutes before slicing and serving.

SWISS CHARD AND POTATO GRATIN

Servings: 4 **Time:** 1 hour

Ingredients:

For the Gratin:

- 1 pound (450g) Swiss chard, stems removed and leaves chopped
- 1 1/2 pounds (680g) potatoes, peeled and thinly sliced
- 1 cup (100g) Swiss cheese (Emmental or Gruyère), grated
- 2 cloves garlic, minced
- 1 cup (240ml) heavy cream
- Salt and black pepper to taste
- 2 tablespoons butter, for greasing

For the Topping:

- 1/4 cup (25g) breadcrumbs
- 2 tablespoons grated Parmesan cheese
- 2 tablespoons fresh parsley, chopped
- 2 tablespoons melted butter

Instructions:

For the Gratin:

1. Preheat your oven to 375°F (190°C).
2. In a large pot of boiling salted water, blanch the Swiss chard leaves for about 1-2 minutes until they wilt. Drain and rinse them with cold water to stop the cooking process. Squeeze out any excess water.
3. In a large mixing bowl, combine the blanched Swiss chard, sliced potatoes, grated Swiss cheese, minced garlic, heavy cream, salt, and black pepper. Toss until the ingredients are well mixed.
4. Grease a baking dish with the 2 tablespoons of butter.

For the Topping:

1. In a separate bowl, mix together the breadcrumbs, grated Parmesan cheese, chopped fresh parsley, and melted butter.

Assembly:

1. Layer the potato and Swiss chard mixture in the greased baking dish, alternating between the two.
2. Sprinkle the breadcrumb topping evenly over the top of the gratin.
3. Cover the baking dish with foil and bake in the preheated oven for about 30 minutes.
4. Remove the foil and bake for an additional 15-20 minutes, or until the gratin is golden brown, the potatoes are tender, and the cream has thickened.
5. Let the Swiss Chard and Potato Gratin rest for a few minutes before serving.

CHEESE-STUFFED PEPPERS

Servings: 4 **Time:** 45 minutes

Ingredients:

- 4 large bell peppers (any color you prefer)
- 1 cup (100g) Swiss cheese (Emmental or Gruyère), grated
- 1/2 cup (50g) breadcrumbs
- 1/4 cup (60ml) milk
- 1/4 cup (30g) grated Parmesan cheese
- 1 small onion, finely chopped
- 2 cloves garlic, minced
- 2 tablespoons fresh parsley, chopped
- 2 tablespoons olive oil
- Salt and black pepper to taste

Instructions:

1. Preheat your oven to 350°F (175°C).
2. Cut the tops off the bell peppers and remove the seeds and membranes from inside.
3. In a bowl, combine the Swiss cheese, breadcrumbs, milk, grated Parmesan cheese, chopped onion, minced garlic, fresh parsley, salt, and black pepper. Mix until the filling is well combined.
4. Stuff each bell pepper with the cheese and breadcrumb mixture, pressing it down gently.
5. Place the stuffed peppers in a baking dish.
6. Drizzle the olive oil over the stuffed peppers.
7. Cover the baking dish with foil.
8. Bake in the preheated oven for about 25-30 minutes.

9. Remove the foil and bake for an additional 10-15 minutes, or until the peppers are tender, and the tops are golden and slightly crispy.
10. Serve the Cheese-Stuffed Peppers hot, as a flavorful and cheesy side or main dish.

SWISS CHEESE AND VEGETABLE TART

Servings: 6 **Time:** 1 hour

Ingredients:

For the Tart Crust:

- 1 1/4 cups (155g) all-purpose flour
- 1/2 teaspoon salt
- 1/2 cup (115g) unsalted butter, cold and cubed
- 3-4 tablespoons ice-cold water

For the Filling:

- 1 cup (100g) Swiss cheese (Emmental or Gruyère), grated
- 1 zucchini, thinly sliced
- 1 red bell pepper, thinly sliced
- 1 yellow bell pepper, thinly sliced
- 1 small red onion, thinly sliced
- 2 cloves garlic, minced
- 2 tablespoons olive oil
- 1 tablespoon fresh thyme leaves
- Salt and black pepper to taste

For the Quiche Custard:

- 4 large eggs
- 1 cup (240ml) heavy cream
- Salt and black pepper to taste
- A pinch of nutmeg (optional)

Instructions:

For the Tart Crust:

1. In a food processor, combine the all-purpose flour and salt.
2. Add the cold, cubed unsalted butter and pulse until the mixture resembles coarse crumbs.
3. Gradually add the ice-cold water and pulse until the dough starts to come together.
4. Turn the dough out onto a floured surface and shape it into a disc.
5. Wrap the dough in plastic wrap and refrigerate for at least 30 minutes.

For the Filling:

1. Preheat your oven to 375°F (190°C).
2. Roll out the chilled tart crust on a floured surface and line a 9-inch (23cm) tart pan with a removable bottom.
3. In a skillet, heat the olive oil over medium heat.
4. Sauté the sliced zucchini, red bell pepper, yellow bell pepper, and red onion until they are slightly softened, about 5-7 minutes.
5. Stir in the minced garlic, fresh thyme leaves, salt, and black pepper. Cook for an additional minute, then remove the skillet from heat.

For the Quiche Custard:

1. In a mixing bowl, whisk together the eggs, heavy cream, salt, black pepper, and nutmeg (if using).

Assembly:

1. Sprinkle the grated Swiss cheese over the prepared tart crust.
2. Arrange the sautéed vegetable mixture over the cheese.
3. Pour the quiche custard over the vegetables and cheese.
4. Place the tart pan on a baking sheet (to catch any potential spills) and bake in the preheated oven for about 30-35 minutes, or until the tart is set and the top is golden brown.
5. Let the Swiss Cheese and Vegetable Tart cool for a few minutes before serving.

SWISS CHEESE AND POTATO BAKE

Servings: 4-6 **Time:** 1 hour

Ingredients:

- 4 cups (about 600g) potatoes, peeled and thinly sliced
- 1 1/2 cups (150g) Swiss cheese (Emmental or Gruyère), grated
- 1/2 cup (120ml) heavy cream
- 1/2 cup (120ml) milk
- 2 cloves garlic, minced
- 2 tablespoons butter

- Salt and black pepper to taste
- A pinch of nutmeg (optional)
- Chopped fresh parsley for garnish (optional)

Instructions:

1. Preheat your oven to 375°F (190°C).
2. In a saucepan, melt the butter over medium heat.
3. Add the minced garlic and sauté for about 1 minute until fragrant.
4. Pour in the heavy cream, milk, and a pinch of nutmeg (if using). Heat the mixture but do not bring it to a boil. Remove from heat.
5. In a greased baking dish, layer half of the thinly sliced potatoes.
6. Sprinkle half of the grated Swiss cheese over the potatoes.
7. Pour half of the cream and milk mixture evenly over the cheese and potatoes.
8. Season with salt and black pepper to taste.
9. Repeat the layering process with the remaining potatoes, Swiss cheese, and cream mixture.
10. Cover the baking dish with foil.
11. Bake in the preheated oven for about 30-35 minutes.
12. Remove the foil and bake for an additional 10-15 minutes, or until the potatoes are tender and the top is golden brown.
13. If desired, garnish with chopped fresh parsley before serving.

DESSERTS

SWISS CHOCOLATE FONDUE

Servings: 4-6 **Time:** 15 minutes

Ingredients:

- 8 ounces (225g) high-quality Swiss dark chocolate (70% cocoa), chopped
- 1 cup (240ml) heavy cream
- 1 tablespoon unsalted butter
- 1 teaspoon pure vanilla extract
- A pinch of salt
- Dipping items (cubed bread, strawberries, bananas, marshmallows, etc.)

Instructions:

1. In a saucepan over low heat, warm the heavy cream until it's just about to simmer. Do not let it boil.
2. Remove the saucepan from the heat and add the chopped Swiss dark chocolate. Let it sit for a minute to allow the chocolate to melt.
3. Gently whisk the chocolate and cream together until the mixture is smooth and silky.
4. Stir in the unsalted butter, pure vanilla extract, and a pinch of salt. Continue to whisk until the mixture is well combined.
5. Transfer the fondue to a fondue pot or a heatproof serving dish. Keep it warm over a low flame or with a tea light candle underneath.
6. Serve the Swiss Chocolate Fondue with an assortment of dipping items, like cubed bread, strawberries, bananas, marshmallows, or any other treats you prefer.
7. Use fondue forks or skewers to dip the items into the warm chocolate fondue, swirling them to coat with the luscious chocolate.
8. Enjoy your Swiss Chocolate Fondue, a delightful dessert that's perfect for sharing!

NUSSTORTE (NUT CAKE)

Servings: 8 **Time:** 1 hour

Ingredients:

For the Pastry:

- 2 1/4 cups (280g) all-purpose flour
- 1/2 cup (120g) unsalted butter, cold and cubed

- 1/2 cup (100g) granulated sugar
- 1 large egg
- 1 teaspoon lemon zest

For the Nut Filling:

- 1 1/2 cups (180g) ground walnuts or hazelnuts
- 1/2 cup (100g) granulated sugar
- 1/2 cup (120ml) heavy cream
- 1 tablespoon honey
- 1 teaspoon cinnamon
- 1/2 teaspoon ground cloves
- 1/4 teaspoon salt

Instructions:

For the Pastry:

1. In a food processor, combine the all-purpose flour, cubed unsalted butter, granulated sugar, and lemon zest.
2. Pulse the ingredients until the mixture resembles coarse crumbs.
3. Add the egg and continue pulsing until the dough starts to come together.
4. Turn the dough out onto a floured surface and shape it into a disc.
5. Wrap the dough in plastic wrap and refrigerate for at least 30 minutes.

For the Nut Filling:

1. In a mixing bowl, combine the ground walnuts or hazelnuts, granulated sugar, heavy cream, honey,

cinnamon, ground cloves, and salt. Mix until the filling is well combined.

Assembly:

1. Preheat your oven to 350°F (175°C).
2. Roll out the chilled pastry on a floured surface to fit a 9-inch (23cm) tart pan with a removable bottom.
3. Place the pastry in the tart pan, pressing it against the bottom and sides.
4. Pour the prepared nut filling into the pastry shell, spreading it evenly.
5. Optionally, use the remaining pastry to create a lattice or decorative top for the nut cake.
6. Bake in the preheated oven for about 25-30 minutes, or until the pastry is golden and the filling is set.
7. Let the Nusstorte cool before serving.

SWISS PLUM TART

Servings: 6-8 **Time:** 1 hour

Ingredients:

For the Tart Crust:

- 1 1/4 cups (155g) all-purpose flour
- 1/4 cup (50g) granulated sugar
- 1/2 cup (115g) unsalted butter, cold and cubed
- 1 large egg yolk

For the Plum Filling:

- 1 1/2 pounds (680g) ripe plums, pitted and sliced
- 1/4 cup (50g) granulated sugar
- 1 teaspoon ground cinnamon
- 1/4 teaspoon ground cloves
- 1 tablespoon lemon juice

For the Topping:

- 1/4 cup (25g) sliced almonds
- 2 tablespoons apricot jam, melted

Instructions:

For the Tart Crust:

1. In a food processor, combine the all-purpose flour, granulated sugar, cubed unsalted butter, and egg yolk.
2. Pulse the ingredients until the mixture resembles coarse crumbs.
3. Turn the dough out onto a floured surface and shape it into a disc.
4. Wrap the dough in plastic wrap and refrigerate for at least 30 minutes.

For the Plum Filling:

1. In a bowl, toss the sliced plums with granulated sugar, ground cinnamon, ground cloves, and lemon juice. Mix until the plums are well coated and allow them to sit for about 15 minutes.

Assembly:

1. Preheat your oven to 375°F (190°C).
2. Roll out the chilled tart crust on a floured surface to fit a 9-inch (23cm) tart pan with a removable bottom.
3. Place the pastry in the tart pan, pressing it against the bottom and sides.
4. Arrange the marinated plum slices in the tart shell, creating an even layer.
5. Sprinkle the sliced almonds over the plums.
6. Bake in the preheated oven for about 30-35 minutes, or until the tart crust is golden and the plums are tender.
7. While the tart is still warm, brush the top with melted apricot jam for a beautiful glaze.
8. Let the Swiss Plum Tart cool before serving.

SWISS LEMON TART

Servings: 8 Time: 1 hour

Ingredients:

For the Tart Crust:

- 1 1/4 cups (155g) all-purpose flour
- 1/4 cup (50g) granulated sugar
- 1/2 cup (115g) unsalted butter, cold and cubed
- 1 large egg yolk

For the Lemon Filling:

- Zest of 2 lemons
- 1/2 cup (120ml) freshly squeezed lemon juice (from about 4 lemons)

- 1 cup (200g) granulated sugar
- 3 large eggs
- 1/2 cup (120ml) heavy cream
- 2 tablespoons cornstarch

For the Topping:

- Powdered sugar for dusting
- Whipped cream or vanilla ice cream (optional)

Instructions:

For the Tart Crust:

1. In a food processor, combine the all-purpose flour, granulated sugar, cubed unsalted butter, and egg yolk.
2. Pulse the ingredients until the mixture resembles coarse crumbs.
3. Turn the dough out onto a floured surface and shape it into a disc.
4. Wrap the dough in plastic wrap and refrigerate for at least 30 minutes.

For the Lemon Filling:

1. Preheat your oven to 350°F (175°C).
2. In a bowl, whisk together the lemon zest, freshly squeezed lemon juice, granulated sugar, eggs, heavy cream, and cornstarch. Mix until the filling is smooth.

Assembly:

1. Roll out the chilled tart crust on a floured surface to fit a 9-inch (23cm) tart pan with a removable bottom.
2. Place the pastry in the tart pan, pressing it against the bottom and sides.
3. Pour the lemon filling into the tart shell.
4. Bake in the preheated oven for about 30-35 minutes, or until the tart is set, and the top is lightly golden.
5. Let the Swiss Lemon Tart cool to room temperature.
6. Dust the top with powdered sugar before serving.
7. Optionally, serve with a dollop of whipped cream or a scoop of vanilla ice cream.

ENGADINER NUSSTORTE (NUT TART FROM ENGADIN)

Servings: 8-10 **Time:** 1 hour

Ingredients:

For the Nut Filling:

- 2 cups (200g) walnuts, coarsely chopped
- 1 cup (200g) granulated sugar
- 1/2 cup (120ml) heavy cream
- 2 tablespoons unsalted butter
- 1 teaspoon vanilla extract
- 1/2 teaspoon ground cinnamon
- A pinch of salt

For the Tart Crust:

- 1 1/4 cups (155g) all-purpose flour
- 1/4 cup (50g) granulated sugar

- 1/2 cup (115g) unsalted butter, cold and cubed
- 1 large egg yolk

Instructions:

For the Nut Filling:

1. In a saucepan, combine the coarsely chopped walnuts, granulated sugar, heavy cream, unsalted butter, vanilla extract, ground cinnamon, and a pinch of salt.
2. Cook the mixture over medium heat, stirring continuously until it thickens and turns into a sticky, caramelized filling. This should take about 10-15 minutes. Remove from heat and let it cool slightly.

For the Tart Crust:

1. In a food processor, combine the all-purpose flour, granulated sugar, cubed unsalted butter, and egg yolk.
2. Pulse the ingredients until the mixture resembles coarse crumbs.
3. Turn the dough out onto a floured surface and shape it into a disc.
4. Wrap the dough in plastic wrap and refrigerate for at least 30 minutes.

Assembly:

1. Preheat your oven to 350°F (175°C).
2. Roll out the chilled tart crust on a floured surface to fit a 9-inch (23cm) tart pan with a removable bottom.

3. Place the pastry in the tart pan, pressing it against the bottom and sides.
4. Pour the caramelized walnut filling into the tart shell.
5. Bake in the preheated oven for about 30-35 minutes, or until the tart is set and the top is golden brown.
6. Let the Engadiner Nusstorte cool before serving.

SWISS APPLE STRUDEL

Servings: 6-8 **Time:** 1 hour

Ingredients:

For the Strudel Dough:

- 2 cups (250g) all-purpose flour
- 1/2 teaspoon salt
- 1/2 cup (120ml) lukewarm water
- 2 tablespoons vegetable oil

For the Apple Filling:

- 4-5 medium apples (e.g., Granny Smith), peeled, cored, and thinly sliced
- 1/2 cup (100g) granulated sugar
- 1 teaspoon ground cinnamon
- 1/4 cup (30g) breadcrumbs
- 1/4 cup (60g) unsalted butter, melted
- 1/2 cup (60g) chopped walnuts or almonds (optional)

For the Topping:

- Powdered sugar for dusting

- Whipped cream or vanilla ice cream (optional)

Instructions:

For the Strudel Dough:

1. In a large bowl, combine the all-purpose flour and salt.
2. Gradually add the lukewarm water and vegetable oil while stirring with a wooden spoon.
3. Knead the dough on a floured surface until it becomes smooth and elastic. Form it into a ball, coat it with a bit of vegetable oil, and let it rest for about 30 minutes, covered with a clean kitchen towel.

For the Apple Filling:

1. In a bowl, combine the thinly sliced apples, granulated sugar, and ground cinnamon. Mix until the apples are well coated.
2. Preheat your oven to 375°F (190°C).

Assembly:

1. Roll out the rested strudel dough on a floured surface into a thin rectangle.
2. Sprinkle the breadcrumbs evenly over the dough, leaving about a 1-inch (2.5cm) border.
3. Arrange the sweetened apple slices over the breadcrumbs.
4. Optionally, drizzle the melted unsalted butter over the apples and sprinkle the chopped walnuts or almonds (if using).

5. Fold in the short sides of the dough to cover the ends of the filling.
6. Carefully roll up the dough from one long side, using the tablecloth or parchment paper to help you roll the strudel. Place it seam-side down on a parchment-lined baking sheet.
7. Bake in the preheated oven for about 30-35 minutes, or until the strudel is golden and the apples are tender.
8. Let the Swiss Apple Strudel cool for a few minutes before serving.
9. Dust the top with powdered sugar and serve slices of strudel with whipped cream or vanilla ice cream if desired.

SWISS CHOCOLATE TRUFFLES

Servings: 20-24 truffles **Time:** 1 hour

Ingredients:

- 8 ounces (225g) high-quality Swiss dark chocolate (70% cocoa), chopped
- 1/2 cup (120ml) heavy cream
- 2 tablespoons unsalted butter
- 1 teaspoon pure vanilla extract
- Cocoa powder, finely chopped nuts, or powdered sugar for coating (optional)

Instructions:

1. Place the chopped Swiss dark chocolate in a heatproof bowl.

2. In a saucepan, heat the heavy cream and unsalted butter over medium heat until it begins to simmer. Do not let it boil.
3. Pour the hot cream mixture over the chopped chocolate.
4. Let it sit for a minute to allow the chocolate to melt, then stir until the mixture is smooth and glossy.
5. Stir in the pure vanilla extract.
6. Cover the bowl and refrigerate the chocolate ganache for about 2 hours or until it firms up.
7. Once the ganache is firm, use a spoon or a melon baller to scoop small portions of the mixture and roll them into balls. If the mixture is too sticky, you can lightly grease your hands with a small amount of butter.
8. Optionally, roll the truffles in cocoa powder, finely chopped nuts, or powdered sugar for coating. Place them on a parchment-lined tray.
9. Refrigerate the coated truffles for about 30 minutes to set.
10. Serve your Swiss Chocolate Truffles as a delightful treat or gift them to someone special.

SWISS MERINGUE

Servings: Varies (enough for topping a pie or cake) **Time:** 15-20 minutes

Ingredients:

- 3 large egg whites
- 3/4 cup (150g) granulated sugar
- 1/4 teaspoon cream of tartar

- 1 teaspoon pure vanilla extract

Instructions:

1. Fill a medium-sized saucepan with a couple of inches of water and bring it to a simmer over medium heat. Once it's simmering, reduce the heat to maintain a gentle simmer.
2. In a heatproof bowl (preferably stainless steel or glass), combine the egg whites, granulated sugar, and cream of tartar.
3. Place the bowl over the simmering water, ensuring that the bottom of the bowl doesn't touch the water. This setup creates a double boiler.
4. Whisk the mixture constantly as it heats. The sugar should dissolve, and the mixture will become warm to the touch. This will take about 4-5 minutes.
5. Remove the bowl from the heat. Using an electric mixer, beat the egg white mixture on high speed until stiff, glossy peaks form. This will take about 5-7 minutes.
6. Stir in the pure vanilla extract and mix until well incorporated.
7. Your Swiss Meringue is now ready to use as a topping for pies, cakes, or any dessert that calls for a light and airy meringue.

SWISS NUT PRALINES

Servings: 20-24 pralines **Time:** 1 hour

Ingredients:

- 1 cup (100g) mixed nuts (e.g., almonds, hazelnuts, walnuts), chopped
- 1/2 cup (120g) granulated sugar
- 2 tablespoons water
- 1/2 teaspoon pure vanilla extract
- A pinch of salt

Instructions:

1. Line a baking sheet with parchment paper and set it aside.
2. In a dry skillet over medium heat, toast the mixed nuts until they become fragrant and slightly browned. Be sure to stir frequently to prevent burning. Remove the toasted nuts from the skillet and set them aside.
3. In a saucepan, combine the granulated sugar and water. Cook over medium-high heat, stirring until the sugar dissolves. Once the mixture starts boiling, stop stirring.
4. Continue to cook the sugar mixture, swirling the pan occasionally, until it reaches a rich amber color. This will take about 5-7 minutes. Keep a close eye on it, as the color can change quickly.
5. Once the caramel is amber, remove the saucepan from the heat.
6. Quickly stir in the chopped nuts, pure vanilla extract, and a pinch of salt. Stir until the nuts are well coated with the caramel.
7. Using a spoon, drop small clusters of the nut mixture onto the prepared baking sheet. You can shape them into praline clusters or simply drop spoonfuls.
8. Let the Swiss Nut Pralines cool and harden at room temperature for about 20-30 minutes.

9. Once they are set, you can enjoy these delicious pralines as a sweet treat or package them as a delightful gift.

BREAKFAST AND BRUNCH

RÜEBLITORTE (CARROT CAKE) PANCAKES

Servings: 4 **Time:** 30 minutes

Ingredients:

For the Pancakes:

- 1 cup (120g) all-purpose flour
- 1 teaspoon baking powder
- 1/2 teaspoon ground cinnamon
- 1/4 teaspoon ground nutmeg
- 1/4 teaspoon salt
- 1/4 cup (50g) granulated sugar
- 1 cup (240ml) buttermilk

- 1 large egg
- 1 cup (100g) grated carrots
- 1/4 cup (30g) chopped walnuts (optional)
- 1/4 cup (30g) raisins (optional)
- Butter or oil for cooking

For the Cream Cheese Drizzle:

- 4 ounces (115g) cream cheese, softened
- 1/4 cup (30g) powdered sugar
- 1/2 teaspoon pure vanilla extract
- 2-3 tablespoons milk

Instructions:

For the Pancakes:

1. In a mixing bowl, whisk together the all-purpose flour, baking powder, ground cinnamon, ground nutmeg, salt, and granulated sugar.
2. In another bowl, combine the buttermilk and the large egg. Mix until well combined.
3. Pour the wet ingredients into the dry ingredients and stir until just combined. Be careful not to overmix; it's okay if there are a few lumps.
4. Gently fold in the grated carrots, chopped walnuts (if using), and raisins (if using).
5. Heat a skillet or griddle over medium-high heat and grease it with a small amount of butter or oil.
6. Pour a ladleful of the pancake batter onto the hot griddle for each pancake. Cook until bubbles form on the surface, then flip and cook until golden brown on both sides.

7. Keep the cooked pancakes warm while you make the cream cheese drizzle.

For the Cream Cheese Drizzle:

1. In a mixing bowl, beat the softened cream cheese until smooth.
2. Add the powdered sugar and pure vanilla extract. Mix until well combined.
3. Gradually add the milk, one tablespoon at a time, until you achieve your desired drizzling consistency.

Assembly:

1. Stack the Rüeblitorte (Carrot Cake) Pancakes on a plate.
2. Drizzle the cream cheese mixture over the pancakes.
3. Optionally, garnish with extra grated carrots, chopped walnuts, or a dusting of powdered sugar.

SWISS BIRCHER MUESLI BOWL

Servings: 2 **Time:** 15 minutes

Ingredients:

For the Muesli:

- 1 cup (90g) rolled oats
- 1 cup (240ml) plain yogurt
- 1/2 cup (120ml) milk (or apple juice)
- 2 tablespoons honey
- 1 apple, grated (leave the skin on)

- 1/4 cup (30g) chopped nuts (e.g., almonds or hazelnuts)
- 1/4 cup (30g) dried fruit (e.g., raisins or apricots), chopped
- A squeeze of fresh lemon juice

For the Toppings:

- Fresh berries (e.g., strawberries, blueberries, raspberries)
- Sliced banana
- Extra chopped nuts
- Honey or maple syrup (optional)

Instructions:

1. In a mixing bowl, combine the rolled oats, plain yogurt, milk (or apple juice), and honey. Mix well.
2. Add the grated apple to the mixture and stir. The lemon juice can be added to the apple to prevent it from browning.
3. Toss in the chopped nuts and dried fruit. Mix until all ingredients are well combined.
4. Divide the Bircher muesli into two serving bowls.
5. Top each bowl with fresh berries, sliced banana, and extra chopped nuts.
6. Optionally, drizzle a bit of honey or maple syrup for extra sweetness.

SWISS CHOCOLATE CROISSANTS

Servings: 6 **Time:** 1 hour

Ingredients:

- 1 sheet of puff pastry (store-bought or homemade)
- 6 ounces (170g) Swiss milk chocolate, broken into 6 pieces
- 1 large egg, beaten (for egg wash)
- Powdered sugar (optional, for dusting)

Instructions:

1. Preheat your oven to 375°F (190°C). Line a baking sheet with parchment paper.
2. Roll out the puff pastry sheet on a lightly floured surface into a large rectangle.
3. Using a sharp knife, cut the rectangle into six smaller rectangles.
4. Place a piece of Swiss milk chocolate at the base of each smaller rectangle.
5. Roll up each rectangle from the base to the tip, enclosing the chocolate.
6. Place the chocolate-filled croissants on the prepared baking sheet with the seam side down.
7. Brush the tops of the croissants with the beaten egg for a golden finish.
8. Bake in the preheated oven for about 20-25 minutes, or until the croissants are puffed up and golden brown.
9. Optionally, dust the Swiss Chocolate Croissants with powdered sugar for a touch of sweetness.
10. Allow the croissants to cool slightly before serving.

SWISS CHEESE BREAKFAST QUICHE

Servings: 6 **Time:** 1 hour

Ingredients:

For the Quiche Crust:

- 1 1/4 cups (155g) all-purpose flour
- 1/2 teaspoon salt
- 1/2 cup (115g) unsalted butter, cold and cubed
- 2-3 tablespoons ice water

For the Quiche Filling:

- 1 cup (100g) shredded Swiss cheese
- 1/2 cup (60g) diced cooked ham or bacon (optional)
- 1/2 cup (60g) diced bell peppers
- 1/2 cup (60g) diced onions
- 4 large eggs
- 1 cup (240ml) milk
- Salt and pepper to taste
- A pinch of ground nutmeg

Instructions:

For the Quiche Crust:

1. In a mixing bowl, combine the all-purpose flour and salt.
2. Add the cold, cubed unsalted butter and use a pastry cutter or your fingers to work it into the flour until the mixture resembles coarse crumbs.
3. Gradually add ice water, one tablespoon at a time, and stir until the dough comes together.

4. Form the dough into a disc, wrap it in plastic wrap, and refrigerate for at least 30 minutes.

For the Quiche Filling:

1. Preheat your oven to 375°F (190°C).
2. In a skillet, sauté the diced bell peppers and onions until they are softened and slightly browned. If using ham or bacon, you can cook and dice it at this point as well.
3. In a separate bowl, whisk together the large eggs, milk, salt, pepper, and a pinch of ground nutmeg.

Assembly:

1. Roll out the chilled quiche crust on a floured surface to fit a 9-inch (23cm) pie or tart pan.
2. Place the pastry in the pan, trimming any excess.
3. Layer the shredded Swiss cheese, sautéed vegetables (and ham or bacon if using) over the pastry.
4. Pour the egg mixture over the filling.
5. Bake in the preheated oven for about 35-40 minutes, or until the quiche is set and the top is golden brown.
6. Let the Swiss Cheese Breakfast Quiche cool for a few minutes before slicing and serving.

SWISS POTATO BREAKFAST HASH

Servings: 4 **Time:** 30 minutes

Ingredients:

- 4 medium potatoes, peeled and diced into 1/2-inch cubes
- 1/2 cup (60g) diced bell peppers (any color)
- 1/2 cup (60g) diced onions
- 1/2 cup (60g) diced ham or bacon (optional)
- 2 tablespoons vegetable oil
- Salt and pepper to taste
- 1 cup (100g) shredded Swiss cheese
- 4 large eggs
- Chopped fresh herbs (e.g., parsley or chives) for garnish (optional)

Instructions:

1. In a large skillet, heat the vegetable oil over medium-high heat.
2. Add the diced potatoes to the skillet and cook, stirring occasionally, until they are golden brown and tender. This will take about 15-20 minutes. Season with salt and pepper to taste.
3. If using, add the diced ham or bacon to the skillet and cook until it's heated through and slightly crispy.
4. Add the diced bell peppers and onions to the skillet and sauté until they are softened and slightly caramelized, about 5-7 minutes.
5. Sprinkle the shredded Swiss cheese over the potato hash and cover the skillet to allow the cheese to melt. This should take about 2-3 minutes.
6. While the cheese is melting, prepare fried or poached eggs in a separate pan or on a griddle.
7. Serve the Swiss Potato Breakfast Hash on plates, and top each portion with a fried or poached egg.

8. Optionally, garnish with chopped fresh herbs like parsley or chives.

SWISS FRUIT AND YOGURT PARFAIT

Servings: 2 **Time:** 10 minutes

Ingredients:

- 1 cup (240g) vanilla or plain yogurt
- 1/2 cup (50g) granola
- 1/2 cup (75g) mixed fresh berries (e.g., strawberries, blueberries, raspberries)
- 1/2 cup (100g) Swiss muesli
- 2 tablespoons honey (optional)
- Fresh mint leaves for garnish (optional)

Instructions:

1. In two serving glasses or bowls, start by layering a spoonful of vanilla or plain yogurt at the bottom.
2. Add a layer of granola on top of the yogurt.
3. Follow with a layer of mixed fresh berries.
4. Add a layer of Swiss muesli.
5. Repeat the layers, starting with yogurt, until the glasses are filled.
6. Optionally, drizzle honey over the top of each parfait for extra sweetness.
7. Garnish with fresh mint leaves for a touch of freshness (optional).
8. Serve your Swiss Fruit and Yogurt Parfait immediately for a delightful and healthy breakfast or snack.

SWISS COOKBOOK

GRILLED AND ROASTED

SWISS GRILLED CHICKEN

Servings: 4 **Time:** 30 minutes

Ingredients:

For the Marinade:

- 1/4 cup (60ml) olive oil
- 2 tablespoons white wine or apple cider vinegar
- 2 cloves garlic, minced
- 1 tablespoon fresh lemon juice
- 1 teaspoon dried thyme
- Salt and black pepper to taste

For the Chicken:

- 4 boneless, skinless chicken breasts
- 1 lemon, cut into wedges (for garnish)

Instructions:

For the Marinade:

1. In a bowl, combine the olive oil, white wine or apple cider vinegar, minced garlic, fresh lemon juice, dried thyme, salt, and black pepper. Mix well.

For the Chicken:

1. Place the boneless, skinless chicken breasts in a resealable plastic bag or a shallow dish.
2. Pour the marinade over the chicken, making sure it's evenly coated. Seal the bag or cover the dish and refrigerate for at least 15 minutes, but longer for better flavor (up to 4 hours).
3. Preheat your grill to medium-high heat.
4. Remove the chicken from the marinade and discard the marinade.
5. Grill the chicken for about 6-7 minutes per side, or until it's cooked through and has grill marks. The internal temperature of the chicken should reach 165°F (74°C).
6. Serve the Swiss Grilled Chicken with lemon wedges for a fresh and zesty garnish.

SWISS ROASTED PORK

Servings: 4-6 **Time:** 2 hours

Ingredients:

For the Roast Pork:

- 2 pounds (900g) boneless pork loin roast
- 2 cloves garlic, minced
- 2 tablespoons olive oil
- 1 teaspoon dried rosemary
- 1 teaspoon dried thyme
- Salt and black pepper to taste

For the Gravy:

- 2 cups (480ml) beef or vegetable broth
- 2 tablespoons all-purpose flour
- Salt and black pepper to taste

Instructions:

For the Roast Pork:

1. Preheat your oven to 350°F (175°C).
2. In a small bowl, mix the minced garlic, olive oil, dried rosemary, dried thyme, salt, and black pepper to create a paste.
3. Make small slits in the pork loin roast with a knife.
4. Rub the garlic and herb paste all over the pork roast, making sure to get it into the slits.
5. Place the seasoned pork roast in a roasting pan.
6. Roast in the preheated oven for about 1 hour and 15 minutes, or until the internal temperature of the pork reaches 145°F (63°C) and the outside is golden brown and crispy.

7. Remove the roast from the oven and let it rest for 10 minutes before slicing.

For the Gravy:

1. In a saucepan, combine the beef or vegetable broth and all-purpose flour. Whisk to dissolve the flour.
2. Cook over medium heat, stirring constantly, until the gravy thickens.
3. Season the gravy with salt and black pepper to taste.

Assembly:

1. Slice the Swiss Roasted Pork and serve it with the gravy.
2. Accompany it with your choice of roasted vegetables or potatoes.

SWISS GRILLED TROUT

Servings: 4 **Time:** 20 minutes

Ingredients:

- 4 whole trout, cleaned and gutted
- 2 tablespoons olive oil
- 2 lemons, sliced into rounds
- 4 sprigs of fresh rosemary
- Salt and black pepper to taste
- Aluminum foil (for grilling)

Instructions:

1. Preheat your grill to medium-high heat.
2. Rinse the cleaned and gutted trout under cold water and pat them dry with paper towels.
3. Season the inside and outside of the trout with salt and black pepper.
4. Stuff the cavity of each trout with lemon slices and a sprig of fresh rosemary.
5. Brush the outside of the trout with olive oil to prevent sticking on the grill.
6. Wrap each trout individually in aluminum foil, ensuring they are well sealed.
7. Place the foil-wrapped trout on the preheated grill and cook for about 7-10 minutes per side. The cooking time may vary depending on the size of the fish and the heat of your grill. The trout should flake easily with a fork when it's done.
8. Carefully remove the foil-wrapped trout from the grill and serve.

GRILLED SWISS SAUSAGES

Servings: 4 **Time:** 20 minutes

Ingredients:

- 4 Swiss sausages (e.g., cervelat or bratwurst)
- 4 crusty bread rolls
- Mustard and ketchup (for serving)
- Pickles and sauerkraut (optional, for serving)

Instructions:

1. Preheat your grill to medium-high heat.

2. Place the Swiss sausages on the grill grates.
3. Grill the sausages for about 8-10 minutes, turning occasionally until they are browned and cooked through. The internal temperature should reach 160°F (71°C).
4. While the sausages are grilling, you can slice the crusty bread rolls in half.
5. Toast the bread rolls on the grill for a minute or two until they are lightly browned.
6. Serve the grilled Swiss sausages in the toasted bread rolls.
7. Offer mustard, ketchup, pickles, and sauerkraut as condiments for everyone to customize their sausages.

SWISS ROAST BEEF

Servings: 6-8 **Time:** 2-3 hours

Ingredients:

- 3-4 pounds (1.5-2 kg) beef roast (e.g., sirloin or rib roast)
- 2 tablespoons olive oil
- 4 cloves garlic, minced
- 2 teaspoons dried rosemary
- Salt and black pepper to taste
- 2 cups (480ml) beef broth
- 1 cup (240ml) dry red wine (optional)
- 2-3 tablespoons all-purpose flour

Instructions:

1. Preheat your oven to 325°F (160°C).

2. In a small bowl, mix the minced garlic, dried rosemary, salt, and black pepper with the olive oil to create a paste.
3. Rub the garlic and herb paste all over the beef roast.
4. Place the roast in a roasting pan with the fat side up.
5. Roast the beef in the preheated oven for about 20 minutes per pound (45 minutes per kg) for medium-rare. Adjust the time for your desired level of doneness. Use a meat thermometer to check the internal temperature; it should be 135°F (57°C) for medium-rare.
6. Remove the roast from the oven and transfer it to a carving board. Cover it with foil and let it rest for at least 15 minutes.
7. In the meantime, prepare the gravy. Pour the pan drippings into a saucepan and add the beef broth and red wine (if using).
8. Heat the mixture over medium heat and bring it to a simmer.
9. In a separate bowl, mix the all-purpose flour with a bit of water to create a slurry. Gradually whisk the slurry into the simmering broth mixture and cook until it thickens into a rich gravy. Season with salt and black pepper to taste.
10. Slice the Swiss Roast Beef and serve it with the gravy.

SWISS ROASTED LAMB

Servings: 4-6 **Time:** 1 hour 30 minutes

Ingredients:

- 3-4 pounds (1.5-2 kg) leg of lamb

- 4 cloves garlic, minced
- 2 tablespoons olive oil
- 2 teaspoons dried rosemary
- Salt and black pepper to taste
- 1 cup (240ml) beef or vegetable broth
- 1/2 cup (120ml) dry white wine (optional)

Instructions:

1. Preheat your oven to 325°F (160°C).
2. In a small bowl, mix the minced garlic, dried rosemary, salt, and black pepper with the olive oil to create a paste.
3. Make small incisions in the leg of lamb with a knife and insert small slivers of garlic into the slits.
4. Rub the garlic and herb paste all over the leg of lamb.
5. Place the lamb in a roasting pan, fat side up.
6. Roast the lamb in the preheated oven for about 20 minutes per pound (45 minutes per kg) for medium-rare. Use a meat thermometer to check the internal temperature; it should be 135°F (57°C) for medium-rare.
7. If desired, you can baste the lamb with the pan juices a few times during the cooking process to keep it moist.
8. Remove the roast from the oven and transfer it to a carving board. Cover it with foil and let it rest for at least 15 minutes.
9. In the meantime, you can make a sauce using the pan drippings. Pour the pan drippings into a saucepan, add the beef or vegetable broth, and white wine (if using).

10. Heat the mixture over medium heat and bring it to a simmer. Reduce it until it reaches the desired consistency for your sauce.
11. Slice the Swiss Roasted Lamb and serve it with the sauce.

PASTA AND RICE

SWISS CHEESE PASTA

Servings: 4 **Time:** 20 minutes

Ingredients:

- 8 ounces (225g) pasta (e.g., macaroni or penne)
- 2 cups (200g) shredded Swiss cheese (e.g., Emmental or Gruyère)
- 1 cup (240ml) whole milk
- 2 tablespoons unsalted butter
- 2 tablespoons all-purpose flour
- 1/4 teaspoon salt
- 1/4 teaspoon black pepper
- 1/4 teaspoon ground nutmeg
- Chopped fresh parsley for garnish (optional)

Instructions:

1. Cook the pasta according to the package instructions until al dente. Drain and set aside.
2. In a saucepan, melt the unsalted butter over medium heat.
3. Stir in the all-purpose flour to create a roux. Cook, stirring constantly, for about 2-3 minutes until the roux is lightly golden.
4. Gradually pour in the whole milk while continuing to stir, ensuring no lumps form.
5. Cook the mixture, stirring, until it thickens into a smooth sauce.
6. Reduce the heat and stir in the shredded Swiss cheese until it's completely melted and the sauce is smooth.
7. Season the sauce with salt, black pepper, and ground nutmeg. Adjust the seasonings to your taste.
8. Combine the cooked pasta with the Swiss cheese sauce.

SWISS CHEESE RISOTTO

Servings: 4 **Time:** 30 minutes

Ingredients:

- 1 1/2 cups (300g) Arborio rice
- 1/2 cup (120ml) dry white wine
- 4 cups (960ml) chicken or vegetable broth
- 1/2 cup (120ml) heavy cream
- 1 cup (100g) shredded Swiss cheese (e.g., Gruyère or Emmental)
- 2 tablespoons unsalted butter

- 1/2 cup (60g) diced onions
- 2 cloves garlic, minced
- Salt and black pepper to taste
- Chopped fresh chives for garnish (optional)

Instructions:

1. In a saucepan, heat the chicken or vegetable broth over low heat to keep it warm.
2. In a large, deep skillet, melt the unsalted butter over medium heat.
3. Add the diced onions and cook until they become translucent, about 3-5 minutes.
4. Stir in the Arborio rice and minced garlic, and cook for an additional 2-3 minutes until the rice is lightly toasted.
5. Pour in the dry white wine and cook until it's mostly absorbed by the rice.
6. Begin adding the warm broth, one ladle at a time, to the rice. Stir constantly and allow the liquid to be absorbed before adding more. Continue this process until the rice is tender and creamy, which should take about 18-20 minutes.
7. Stir in the heavy cream and shredded Swiss cheese until the cheese is melted, and the risotto is creamy.
8. Season the risotto with salt and black pepper to taste.

SWISS CHEESE AND MUSHROOM PASTA

Servings: 4 **Time:** 25 minutes

Ingredients:

- 8 ounces (225g) pasta (e.g., fettuccine or penne)
- 2 tablespoons unsalted butter
- 8 ounces (225g) sliced mushrooms
- 2 cloves garlic, minced
- 1 cup (240ml) heavy cream
- 1 cup (100g) shredded Swiss cheese (e.g., Emmental or Gruyère)
- Salt and black pepper to taste
- Chopped fresh parsley for garnish (optional)

Instructions:

1. Cook the pasta according to the package instructions until al dente. Drain and set aside.
2. In a large skillet, melt the unsalted butter over medium heat.
3. Add the sliced mushrooms and sauté until they become tender and browned, about 5-7 minutes.
4. Stir in the minced garlic and cook for an additional minute until fragrant.
5. Pour in the heavy cream and bring the mixture to a simmer. Cook for about 3-4 minutes, allowing the cream to thicken.
6. Reduce the heat and add the shredded Swiss cheese. Stir until the cheese is completely melted and the sauce is smooth.
7. Season the sauce with salt and black pepper to taste.
8. Add the cooked pasta to the skillet and toss to coat it with the Swiss cheese and mushroom sauce.

SWISS CHEESE AND HAM PASTA

Servings: 4 **Time:** 20 minutes

Ingredients:

- 8 ounces (225g) pasta (e.g., penne or rotini)
- 1 cup (240ml) heavy cream
- 1 cup (100g) shredded Swiss cheese (e.g., Emmental or Gruyère)
- 1/2 cup (60g) diced ham
- 2 tablespoons unsalted butter
- 1 clove garlic, minced
- Salt and black pepper to taste
- Chopped fresh parsley for garnish (optional)

Instructions:

1. Cook the pasta according to the package instructions until al dente. Drain and set aside.
2. In a large skillet, melt the unsalted butter over medium heat.
3. Add the diced ham to the skillet and sauté for a few minutes until it starts to brown.
4. Stir in the minced garlic and cook for an additional minute until fragrant.
5. Pour in the heavy cream and bring it to a simmer. Cook for about 3-4 minutes, allowing the cream to thicken.
6. Reduce the heat and add the shredded Swiss cheese. Stir until the cheese is completely melted and the sauce is smooth.
7. Season the sauce with salt and black pepper to taste.
8. Add the cooked pasta to the skillet and toss to coat it with the Swiss cheese and ham sauce.

SWISS RICE PUDDING

Servings: 4 **Time:** 1 hour

Ingredients:

- 1/2 cup (100g) Arborio rice
- 4 cups (960ml) whole milk
- 1/2 cup (100g) granulated sugar
- 1/2 teaspoon vanilla extract
- 1/4 teaspoon ground cinnamon
- A pinch of salt
- 1/4 cup (25g) raisins (optional)
- Ground cinnamon or nutmeg for garnish (optional)

Instructions:

1. In a medium saucepan, combine the Arborio rice and whole milk.
2. Bring the mixture to a gentle simmer over medium heat, stirring frequently.
3. Reduce the heat to low, cover the saucepan, and let the rice cook for about 30-35 minutes, or until it's tender and the mixture has thickened.
4. Stir in the granulated sugar, vanilla extract, ground cinnamon, and a pinch of salt. If you're using raisins, add them at this point.
5. Continue to cook the rice pudding for an additional 10-15 minutes, or until it reaches your desired consistency. Remember that it will thicken further as it cools.
6. Remove the saucepan from heat and let the rice pudding cool slightly.
7. If desired, sprinkle ground cinnamon or nutmeg on top for garnish.

8. Serve your Swiss Rice Pudding warm or chilled.

SWISS RICE AND VEGETABLE PILAF

Servings: 4 **Time:** 30 minutes

Ingredients:

- 1 cup (200g) long-grain rice
- 2 cups (480ml) vegetable broth
- 1/2 cup (100g) frozen peas
- 1/2 cup (100g) diced carrots
- 1/2 cup (100g) diced bell peppers (any color)
- 1/2 cup (100g) diced zucchini
- 1/2 cup (100g) diced Swiss cheese (e.g., Emmental or Gruyère)
- 2 tablespoons olive oil
- 1 teaspoon dried thyme
- Salt and black pepper to taste
- Chopped fresh parsley for garnish (optional)

Instructions:

1. Rinse the rice in cold water until the water runs clear, and then drain it.
2. In a large skillet or pan, heat the olive oil over medium heat.
3. Add the rice and sauté for about 2-3 minutes until it becomes lightly toasted.
4. Pour in the vegetable broth and bring it to a boil.
5. Reduce the heat, cover, and let the rice simmer for about 10 minutes.

6. Stir in the frozen peas, diced carrots, bell peppers, and zucchini.
7. Cover the pan and continue to simmer for an additional 10-15 minutes, or until the rice is tender and the vegetables are cooked.
8. Stir in the diced Swiss cheese until it's melted and the pilaf is creamy.
9. Season the pilaf with dried thyme, salt, and black pepper to taste.

SNACKS AND FINGER FOODS

SWISS CHEESE BITES

Servings: 4 **Time:** 15 minutes

Ingredients:

- 1 sheet of frozen puff pastry, thawed
- 1/2 cup (50g) shredded Swiss cheese (e.g., Emmental or Gruyère)
- 1/4 cup (25g) grated Parmesan cheese
- 1 egg, beaten (for egg wash)
- Sesame seeds or poppy seeds for sprinkling (optional)

Instructions:

1. Preheat your oven to 400°F (200°C) and line a baking sheet with parchment paper.
2. Roll out the thawed puff pastry sheet on a lightly floured surface to smooth out any creases.
3. Sprinkle the shredded Swiss cheese and grated Parmesan cheese evenly over the pastry sheet.
4. Gently press the cheese into the pastry with a rolling pin to help it adhere.
5. Fold the pastry sheet in half, sandwiching the cheese inside.
6. Brush the top of the pastry with the beaten egg to create a shiny finish.
7. If desired, sprinkle sesame seeds or poppy seeds on top.
8. Cut the pastry into bite-sized squares or rectangles.
9. Transfer the Swiss Cheese Bites to the prepared baking sheet.
10. Bake in the preheated oven for about 10-12 minutes or until the bites are puffed up and golden brown.
11. Allow them to cool slightly before serving.

SWISS CHEESE AND HAM BITES

Servings: 4 **Time:** 20 minutes

Ingredients:

- 1 sheet of frozen puff pastry, thawed
- 1/2 cup (50g) shredded Swiss cheese (e.g., Emmental or Gruyère)
- 1/4 cup (25g) diced ham
- 1 egg, beaten (for egg wash)
- Sesame seeds or poppy seeds for sprinkling (optional)

Instructions:

1. Preheat your oven to 400°F (200°C) and line a baking sheet with parchment paper.
2. Roll out the thawed puff pastry sheet on a lightly floured surface to smooth out any creases.
3. Sprinkle the shredded Swiss cheese and diced ham evenly over the pastry sheet.
4. Gently press the cheese and ham into the pastry with a rolling pin to help them adhere.
5. Fold the pastry sheet in half, sandwiching the cheese and ham inside.
6. Brush the top of the pastry with the beaten egg to create a shiny finish.
7. If desired, sprinkle sesame seeds or poppy seeds on top.
8. Cut the pastry into bite-sized squares or rectangles.
9. Transfer the Swiss Cheese and Ham Bites to the prepared baking sheet.
10. Bake in the preheated oven for about 10-12 minutes or until the bites are puffed up and golden brown.
11. Allow them to cool slightly before serving.

SWISS CHEESE STRAWS

Servings: 4 **Time:** 30 minutes

Ingredients:

- 1 sheet of frozen puff pastry, thawed
- 1/2 cup (50g) shredded Swiss cheese (e.g., Emmental or Gruyère)
- 1/4 cup (25g) grated Parmesan cheese

- 1 egg, beaten (for egg wash)
- Sesame seeds or poppy seeds for sprinkling (optional)

Instructions:

1. Preheat your oven to 400°F (200°C) and line a baking sheet with parchment paper.
2. Roll out the thawed puff pastry sheet on a lightly floured surface to smooth out any creases.
3. Sprinkle the shredded Swiss cheese and grated Parmesan cheese evenly over the pastry sheet.
4. Gently press the cheese into the pastry with a rolling pin to help it adhere.
5. Fold the pastry sheet in half, sandwiching the cheese inside.
6. Brush the top of the pastry with the beaten egg to create a shiny finish.
7. If desired, sprinkle sesame seeds or poppy seeds on top.
8. Using a sharp knife or a pizza cutter, cut the pastry into long, thin strips, about 1/2 inch (1.3 cm) wide.
9. Carefully twist each strip a few times to create the straws.
10. Transfer the Swiss Cheese Straws to the prepared baking sheet.
11. Bake in the preheated oven for about 12-15 minutes or until the straws are puffed up and golden brown.
12. Allow them to cool slightly before serving.

SWISS ROASTED NUTS

Servings: 4 **Time:** 15 minutes

Ingredients:

- 2 cups (300g) mixed nuts (e.g., almonds, walnuts, cashews)
- 2 tablespoons unsalted butter, melted
- 1 tablespoon honey
- 1/2 teaspoon salt
- 1/4 teaspoon ground cinnamon

Instructions:

1. Preheat your oven to 350°F (175°C) and line a baking sheet with parchment paper.
2. In a microwave-safe bowl, melt the unsalted butter.
3. Stir in the honey, salt, and ground cinnamon into the melted butter.
4. In a large bowl, combine the mixed nuts with the butter and honey mixture. Toss to coat the nuts evenly.
5. Spread the coated nuts in a single layer on the prepared baking sheet.
6. Roast the nuts in the preheated oven for about 10-12 minutes, stirring once or twice, until they are golden and fragrant.
7. Remove the Swiss Roasted Nuts from the oven and let them cool on the baking sheet.
8. Once completely cool, transfer them to an airtight container for storage.

SWISS CHEESE AND TOMATO SKEWERS

Servings: 4 **Time:** 15 minutes

Ingredients:

- 12 cherry tomatoes
- 12 cubes of Swiss cheese (e.g., Emmental or Gruyère)
- 12 fresh basil leaves
- 2 tablespoons balsamic glaze
- Wooden skewers or toothpicks

Instructions:

1. Assemble your skewers by threading a cherry tomato, a cube of Swiss cheese, and a fresh basil leaf onto each skewer or toothpick.
2. Arrange the Swiss Cheese and Tomato Skewers on a serving platter.
3. Drizzle the balsamic glaze over the skewers just before serving.

SWISS CHEESE AND ONION TARTLETS

Servings: 4 **Time:** 45 minutes

Ingredients:

For the Tartlet Shells:

- 1 sheet of frozen puff pastry, thawed
- Cooking spray or butter for greasing

For the Filling:

- 2 large onions, thinly sliced
- 2 tablespoons unsalted butter

- 1/2 cup (50g) shredded Swiss cheese (e.g., Emmental or Gruyère)
- 1/4 cup (60ml) heavy cream
- 1 egg
- Salt and black pepper to taste
- Fresh thyme leaves for garnish (optional)

Instructions:

1. Preheat your oven to 400°F (200°C) and grease four small tartlet or muffin cups with cooking spray or butter.

Making the Tartlet Shells:

1. Roll out the thawed puff pastry sheet on a lightly floured surface.
2. Cut the puff pastry into four squares or circles, depending on the shape of your tartlet cups.
3. Gently press the puff pastry squares or circles into the greased tartlet cups.
4. Use a fork to prick the bottom of the pastry to prevent it from puffing up too much during baking.

Making the Filling:

1. In a skillet, melt the unsalted butter over medium heat.
2. Add the thinly sliced onions and sauté for about 15-20 minutes until they become golden and caramelized. Set them aside to cool.
3. In a bowl, whisk together the egg and heavy cream. Season with salt and black pepper to taste.

4. Distribute the caramelized onions evenly among the puff pastry shells.
5. Sprinkle the shredded Swiss cheese over the onions.
6. Pour the egg and cream mixture over the onions and cheese.

Baking the Tartlets:

1. Place the tartlet cups on a baking sheet and bake in the preheated oven for about 20-25 minutes, or until the tartlets are puffed up and golden brown.
2. Optionally, garnish with fresh thyme leaves for added flavor and presentation.

SWISS CHEESE STUFFED PEPPERS

Servings: 4 **Time:** 1 hour

Ingredients:

- 4 large bell peppers (any color)
- 1 cup (100g) shredded Swiss cheese (e.g., Emmental or Gruyère)
- 1 cup (200g) cooked rice
- 1/2 cup (120ml) tomato sauce
- 1/2 cup (120ml) vegetable or chicken broth
- 1/2 cup (75g) diced onions
- 1 clove garlic, minced
- 1 tablespoon olive oil
- 1 teaspoon dried oregano
- Salt and black pepper to taste
- Fresh parsley for garnish (optional)

Instructions:

1. Preheat your oven to 375°F (190°C).
2. Cut the tops off the bell peppers and remove the seeds and membranes. If necessary, trim the bottoms slightly to make them stand upright.
3. In a skillet, heat the olive oil over medium heat.
4. Add the diced onions and minced garlic, and sauté for about 3-5 minutes until they become translucent.
5. Stir in the cooked rice, shredded Swiss cheese, dried oregano, salt, and black pepper. Mix until the cheese is melted and the filling is well combined.
6. Stuff the bell peppers with the Swiss cheese and rice mixture.
7. Place the stuffed peppers in a baking dish.
8. In a small bowl, mix the tomato sauce and vegetable or chicken broth.
9. Pour the tomato sauce mixture over the stuffed peppers.
10. Cover the baking dish with aluminum foil.
11. Bake in the preheated oven for 30-35 minutes, or until the peppers are tender.
12. Optionally, garnish with fresh parsley before serving.

SWEETS AND TREATS

SWISS CHOCOLATE BROWNIES

Servings: 12 Time: 35 minutes

Ingredients:

- 1/2 cup (115g) unsalted butter
- 4 ounces (115g) Swiss chocolate (dark or milk), chopped
- 1 cup (200g) granulated sugar
- 2 large eggs
- 1 teaspoon vanilla extract
- 1/2 cup (60g) all-purpose flour
- 1/4 cup (30g) unsweetened cocoa powder
- 1/4 teaspoon salt
- 1/2 cup (60g) chopped nuts (optional)

Instructions:

1. Preheat your oven to 350°F (175°C) and line an 8x8-inch (20x20cm) square baking pan with parchment paper.
2. In a microwave-safe bowl, melt the unsalted butter and chopped Swiss chocolate together in 30-second intervals, stirring until smooth. Alternatively, you can use a double boiler for this step.
3. Once melted and smooth, let the chocolate mixture cool slightly.
4. Stir in the granulated sugar until well combined.
5. Add the eggs one at a time, mixing well after each addition.
6. Stir in the vanilla extract.
7. In a separate bowl, whisk together the all-purpose flour, unsweetened cocoa powder, and salt.
8. Gradually add the dry mixture to the chocolate mixture, stirring until just combined. Do not overmix.
9. If you're using chopped nuts, fold them into the batter.
10. Pour the brownie batter into the prepared baking pan and spread it evenly.
11. Bake in the preheated oven for 25-30 minutes, or until a toothpick inserted into the center comes out with a few moist crumbs.
12. Allow the Swiss Chocolate Brownies to cool completely in the pan.
13. Once cooled, remove the brownies from the pan using the parchment paper as handles.
14. Cut into squares and serve.

SWISS FRUIT COMPOTE

Servings: 4 Time: 20 minutes

Ingredients:

- 4 cups (600g) mixed fresh fruits (e.g., apples, pears, berries, or any of your favorites)
- 1/4 cup (50g) granulated sugar
- 1/2 cup (120ml) water
- 1/2 teaspoon vanilla extract
- 1 lemon, zest and juice

Instructions:

1. Wash, peel (if necessary), and dice the fresh fruits into bite-sized pieces.
2. In a saucepan, combine the diced fruits, granulated sugar, water, and the zest and juice of the lemon.
3. Bring the mixture to a gentle simmer over medium heat.
4. Reduce the heat to low and let the fruits simmer for about 10-15 minutes, or until they are soft and the sugar has dissolved.
5. Stir in the vanilla extract.
6. Remove the Swiss Fruit Compote from the heat and let it cool slightly.
7. Serve the compote warm or at room temperature as a topping for ice cream, yogurt, pancakes, or as a simple, sweet dessert.

SWISS APPLE CRUMBLE

Servings: 6 Time: 45 minutes

Ingredients:

For the Apple Filling:

- 4-5 medium apples, peeled, cored, and sliced
- 1/4 cup (50g) granulated sugar
- 1 tablespoon lemon juice
- 1 teaspoon ground cinnamon
- 1/4 teaspoon ground nutmeg
- 1/4 teaspoon salt

For the Crumble Topping:

- 1 cup (120g) all-purpose flour
- 1/2 cup (100g) granulated sugar
- 1/2 cup (115g) unsalted butter, cold and cubed
- 1/4 teaspoon salt

Instructions:

Making the Apple Filling:

1. Preheat your oven to 350°F (175°C) and grease a baking dish.
2. In a large bowl, combine the sliced apples, granulated sugar, lemon juice, ground cinnamon, ground nutmeg, and salt. Toss to coat the apples evenly.
3. Transfer the apple mixture to the greased baking dish.

Making the Crumble Topping:

1. In a separate bowl, combine the all-purpose flour, granulated sugar, and salt.
2. Add the cold, cubed unsalted butter to the dry ingredients.
3. Use a pastry cutter or your fingers to work the butter into the dry ingredients until the mixture resembles coarse crumbs.

Assembling and Baking:

1. Sprinkle the crumble topping evenly over the apple filling in the baking dish.
2. Bake in the preheated oven for about 30-35 minutes, or until the crumble topping is golden brown and the apple filling is bubbling.
3. Remove the Swiss Apple Crumble from the oven and let it cool slightly before serving.
4. Serve warm with a scoop of vanilla ice cream or a dollop of whipped cream, if desired.

SWISS CARAMEL PUDDING

Servings: 4 Time: 1 hour (including chilling time)

Ingredients:

For the Caramel Sauce:

- 1/2 cup (100g) granulated sugar
- 2 tablespoons water

For the Pudding:

- 2 cups (480ml) whole milk
- 1/2 cup (100g) granulated sugar
- 4 large eggs
- 1 teaspoon vanilla extract

Instructions:

Making the Caramel Sauce:

1. In a saucepan, combine the granulated sugar and water.
2. Heat the mixture over medium-high heat, swirling the pan occasionally, until it turns into a deep amber caramel. Be careful not to stir, but you can gently swirl the pan to ensure even caramelization.
3. Once the caramel reaches the desired color, immediately pour it into the bottom of four ramekins or pudding cups. Tilt and rotate the cups to spread the caramel evenly over the bottoms. Let it cool and harden.

Making the Pudding:

1. Preheat your oven to 325°F (160°C).
2. In a separate saucepan, heat the whole milk over medium heat until it's warm but not boiling. Remove it from the heat and let it cool slightly.
3. In a bowl, whisk together the granulated sugar, eggs, and vanilla extract until well combined.
4. Gradually whisk the warm milk into the egg mixture.
5. Pour the custard mixture into the caramel-coated ramekins.

Baking:

1. Place the ramekins in a baking dish and fill the dish with enough hot water to reach halfway up the sides of the ramekins. This creates a water bath.
2. Carefully transfer the baking dish to the preheated oven.
3. Bake for about 30-35 minutes, or until the puddings are set but slightly jiggly in the center.
4. Remove the baking dish from the oven and let the puddings cool in the water bath.

5. Once cooled, refrigerate the Swiss Caramel Puddings for at least a few hours or until they are well chilled.
6. To serve, run a knife around the edge of each ramekin and invert the pudding onto a plate, allowing the caramel to drizzle over the top.

SWISS HAZELNUT BRITTLE

Servings: Varies (depends on portion size) Time: 30 minutes

Ingredients:

- 1 cup (200g) granulated sugar
- 1 cup (140g) whole hazelnuts
- 1/4 cup (60ml) water
- 1/4 teaspoon salt
- 1/2 teaspoon vanilla extract
- 1/4 teaspoon baking soda

Instructions:

1. Prepare a baking sheet by lining it with parchment paper and lightly greasing it. Set it aside.
2. In a heavy-bottomed saucepan, combine the granulated sugar and water over medium heat. Stir until the sugar dissolves, and then stop stirring.
3. Continue to cook the sugar mixture, swirling the pan occasionally, until it turns a deep amber color. This can take about 10-15 minutes. Be cautious as caramel can go from perfect to burnt quickly.
4. Once the caramel reaches the desired color, remove the saucepan from the heat, and quickly stir in the salt,

vanilla extract, and baking soda. The mixture will bubble up, so be cautious.
5. Immediately stir in the whole hazelnuts, coating them evenly with the caramel.
6. Pour the caramel-coated hazelnuts onto the prepared baking sheet.
7. Use a greased spatula or the back of a greased spoon to quickly spread out the mixture and flatten it to your desired thickness.
8. Let the Swiss Hazelnut Brittle cool and harden at room temperature for about 20-30 minutes.
9. Once completely cooled and hardened, break the brittle into pieces. You can do this by tapping it gently with a rolling pin or by simply snapping it into shards.
10. Store the brittle in an airtight container.

SWISS MERINGUE COOKIES

Servings: Varies (depends on portion size) Time: 2 hours (including cooling time)

Ingredients:

- 4 large egg whites
- 1 cup (200g) granulated sugar
- 1 teaspoon vanilla extract
- A pinch of salt

Instructions:

1. Preheat your oven to 200°F (95°C) and line a baking sheet with parchment paper.

2. In a heatproof bowl, combine the egg whites and granulated sugar.
3. Create a double boiler by placing the bowl over a pot of simmering water (make sure the bottom of the bowl doesn't touch the water). Whisk the egg whites and sugar constantly until the mixture reaches a temperature of 160°F (71°C) and the sugar has completely dissolved. This step will take about 5-7 minutes.
4. Remove the bowl from the heat and wipe the bottom to prevent any water droplets from getting into the mixture.
5. Use an electric mixer (handheld or stand mixer) to beat the egg white mixture on high speed until stiff, glossy peaks form. This should take about 5-7 minutes.
6. Gently fold in the vanilla extract and a pinch of salt. Be careful not to deflate the meringue.
7. Transfer the meringue mixture to a piping bag fitted with a star or round tip, or simply drop spoonfuls onto the parchment-lined baking sheet.
8. Bake in the preheated oven for 1.5-2 hours, or until the meringue cookies are dry and crisp on the outside.
9. Turn off the oven and leave the meringues in the oven for an additional hour to cool and dry completely.
10. Once cooled, remove the Swiss Meringue Cookies from the baking sheet and store them in an airtight container.

SWISS NUT BRITTLE

Servings: Varies (depends on portion size) Time: 20 minutes

Ingredients:

- 1 cup (200g) granulated sugar

- 1/2 cup (60g) mixed nuts (e.g., almonds, walnuts, cashews)
- 1/4 cup (60ml) water
- 1/4 teaspoon salt
- 1/2 teaspoon vanilla extract
- 1/4 teaspoon baking soda

Instructions:

1. Prepare a baking sheet by lining it with parchment paper and lightly greasing it. Set it aside.
2. In a heavy-bottomed saucepan, combine the granulated sugar and water over medium heat. Stir until the sugar dissolves, and then stop stirring.
3. Continue to cook the sugar mixture, swirling the pan occasionally, until it turns a deep amber color. This can take about 10-15 minutes. Be cautious as caramel can go from perfect to burnt quickly.
4. Once the caramel reaches the desired color, remove the saucepan from the heat, and quickly stir in the salt, vanilla extract, and baking soda. The mixture will bubble up, so be cautious.
5. Immediately stir in the mixed nuts, coating them evenly with the caramel.
6. Pour the caramel-coated nuts onto the prepared baking sheet.
7. Use a greased spatula or the back of a greased spoon to quickly spread out the mixture and flatten it to your desired thickness.
8. Let the Swiss Nut Brittle cool and harden at room temperature for about 20-30 minutes.
9. Once completely cooled and hardened, break the brittle into pieces. You can do this by tapping it gently with a rolling pin or by simply snapping it into shards.

10. Store the brittle in an airtight container.

SWISS CHOCOLATE HAZELNUT SPREAD

Servings: About 2 cups **Time:** 20 minutes

Ingredients:

- 1 cup (140g) hazelnuts
- 1/2 cup (60g) powdered sugar
- 1/4 cup (30g) unsweetened cocoa powder
- 1/4 cup (60ml) vegetable oil
- 1 teaspoon vanilla extract
- A pinch of salt

Instructions:

1. Preheat your oven to 350°F (175°C).
2. Place the hazelnuts on a baking sheet in a single layer and toast them in the preheated oven for about 10-12 minutes or until they become fragrant and their skins start to loosen.
3. Remove the hazelnuts from the oven and let them cool slightly. Once they are cool enough to handle, rub them between your hands or in a clean kitchen towel to remove as much of the skin as possible.
4. In a food processor, pulse the skinned hazelnuts until they turn into a smooth hazelnut butter. This can take a few minutes. Scrape down the sides of the food processor bowl as needed.
5. Add the powdered sugar, unsweetened cocoa powder, vegetable oil, vanilla extract, and a pinch of salt to the hazelnut butter in the food processor.

6. Process the mixture until it becomes a smooth and creamy chocolate hazelnut spread. This may take a few more minutes.
7. Taste and adjust the sweetness or saltiness as desired by adding more powdered sugar or a pinch of salt, if needed.
8. Transfer the Swiss Chocolate Hazelnut Spread to a clean jar or airtight container.

HOLIDAY SPECIALS

SWISS CHRISTMAS COOKIES

Servings: Varies (depends on cookie size) Time: 2 hours

Ingredients:

For the Cookies:

- 2 cups (250g) all-purpose flour
- 1/2 cup (60g) ground almonds
- 1/2 cup (60g) confectioners' sugar
- 1 cup (225g) unsalted butter, softened
- 1 large egg yolk
- 1 teaspoon vanilla extract
- 1/2 teaspoon almond extract
- A pinch of salt

For the Glaze:

- 1 cup (120g) confectioners' sugar
- 2-3 tablespoons milk
- Assorted sprinkles or colored sugar for decorating (optional)

Instructions:

Making the Cookies:

1. In a bowl, whisk together the all-purpose flour and ground almonds. Set aside.
2. In a separate bowl, cream the softened unsalted butter and confectioners' sugar together until light and fluffy.
3. Add the egg yolk, vanilla extract, almond extract, and a pinch of salt. Mix until well combined.
4. Gradually add the dry mixture of flour and ground almonds to the wet ingredients. Mix until a soft dough forms.
5. Divide the dough in half and shape each half into a disc. Wrap them in plastic wrap and refrigerate for about 30 minutes.
6. Preheat your oven to 350°F (175°C) and line baking sheets with parchment paper.
7. Roll out one of the dough discs on a lightly floured surface to about 1/4-inch (0.5cm) thickness.
8. Use festive cookie cutters to cut out your desired shapes. Transfer the cookies to the prepared baking sheets.

9. Bake in the preheated oven for 8-10 minutes, or until the cookies are just starting to turn golden around the edges.
10. Remove the cookies from the oven and let them cool on the baking sheets for a few minutes before transferring them to wire racks to cool completely.

Making the Glaze:

1. In a bowl, mix the confectioners' sugar with enough milk to make a smooth and slightly thick glaze.
2. Dip the cooled cookies into the glaze, letting any excess drip off.
3. Place the glazed cookies on a wire rack and decorate them with assorted sprinkles or colored sugar, if desired.
4. Let the glaze set before storing or serving.

SWISS EASTER BREAD

Servings: 1 large loaf Time: 3 hours

Ingredients:

For the Bread:

- 3 1/2 cups (440g) all-purpose flour
- 1/2 cup (100g) granulated sugar
- 1 packet (7g) active dry yeast
- 1/2 cup (120ml) warm milk
- 1/2 cup (120ml) warm water
- 1/4 cup (60g) unsalted butter, melted
- 2 large eggs

- 1 teaspoon vanilla extract
- 1/2 teaspoon salt
- 1/2 cup (100g) raisins
- 1/4 cup (30g) candied citron peel (optional)
- 1 hard-boiled colored egg for decoration (optional)

For the Glaze:

- 1/2 cup (60g) powdered sugar
- 1-2 tablespoons milk
- Sprinkles or colored sugar for decorating (optional)

Instructions:

Making the Dough:

1. In a small bowl, dissolve the active dry yeast in warm water. Let it sit for about 5-10 minutes, or until it becomes frothy.
2. In a large mixing bowl, combine the warm milk, melted unsalted butter, and granulated sugar. Mix until the sugar is dissolved.
3. Add the frothy yeast mixture, eggs, and vanilla extract to the bowl. Mix until well combined.
4. Gradually add the all-purpose flour and salt to the wet ingredients, mixing until a soft dough forms.
5. Knead the dough on a floured surface for about 5-10 minutes, or until it becomes smooth and elastic.
6. Place the dough in a greased bowl, cover it with a clean kitchen towel, and let it rise in a warm place for about 1 hour or until it has doubled in size.

Shaping and Decorating:

1. Punch down the risen dough to release the air.
2. Knead in the raisins and candied citron peel, if using.
3. Shape the dough into a round loaf. If desired, gently press a hard-boiled colored egg into the center of the loaf for decoration.
4. Place the shaped loaf on a parchment-lined baking sheet and cover it with a kitchen towel. Let it rise for another 30-45 minutes.

Baking:

1. Preheat your oven to 350°F (175°C).
2. Bake the Swiss Easter Bread in the preheated oven for 25-30 minutes, or until it's golden brown and sounds hollow when tapped on the bottom.
3. Remove the bread from the oven and let it cool on a wire rack.

Making the Glaze:

1. In a small bowl, mix the powdered sugar with enough milk to make a thick, but pourable glaze.
2. Once the bread has cooled, drizzle the glaze over the top.
3. Decorate with sprinkles or colored sugar, if desired.

SWISS CHEESE FONDUE FOR NEW YEAR'S

Servings: 4-6 Time: 30 minutes

Ingredients:

- 1 clove garlic, peeled

- 1 1/2 cups (350ml) dry white wine
- 1 teaspoon lemon juice
- 1/2 pound (225g) Gruyère cheese, grated
- 1/2 pound (225g) Emmental cheese, grated
- 2 tablespoons all-purpose flour
- 1/4 teaspoon freshly ground white pepper
- A pinch of freshly grated nutmeg
- 1 French baguette, cut into bite-sized cubes
- 1 tablespoon Kirsch (Swiss cherry brandy, optional)
- 1 pinch of salt, to taste

Instructions:

1. Rub the inside of a fondue pot with the peeled garlic clove and then discard the garlic.
2. Pour the white wine and lemon juice into the fondue pot and heat it gently over low heat. Be careful not to let it boil.
3. In a separate bowl, combine the grated Gruyère and Emmental cheese with the all-purpose flour, ensuring the cheese is coated evenly.
4. Gradually add the cheese mixture to the warm wine, stirring constantly until the cheese is melted and the mixture becomes smooth.
5. Stir in the freshly ground white pepper, a pinch of freshly grated nutmeg, and the optional Kirsch if desired.
6. If the fondue is too thick, you can adjust the consistency by adding a bit more white wine.
7. Taste the fondue and add a pinch of salt if needed, although the cheese is already naturally salty.
8. Place the fondue pot over a flame or a fondue burner at the table to keep the mixture warm.

9. Serve with the bite-sized cubes of French baguette for dipping. Each person can spear a piece of bread on a long fork and dip it into the cheese, swirling it to coat.

SWISS THANKSGIVING PIE

Servings: 8-10 Time: 1 hour and 30 minutes

Ingredients:

For the Crust:

- 1 1/4 cups (160g) all-purpose flour
- 1/2 teaspoon salt
- 1/2 cup (115g) unsalted butter, cold and cubed
- 3-4 tablespoons ice water

For the Filling:

- 3/4 cup (150g) granulated sugar
- 2 large eggs
- 1 cup (240ml) heavy cream
- 1/4 cup (60ml) whole milk
- 1 teaspoon vanilla extract
- 1/2 teaspoon ground cinnamon
- 1/4 teaspoon ground nutmeg
- 1/4 teaspoon salt
- 1 1/2 cups (375g) cooked and mashed butternut squash (or canned puree)

For the Topping:

- 1/2 cup (70g) chopped walnuts
- 1/4 cup (30g) brown sugar

- 1/4 cup (30g) all-purpose flour
- 1/4 cup (60g) unsalted butter, softened

Instructions:

Making the Crust:

1. In a food processor, combine the all-purpose flour and salt. Pulse a couple of times to mix.
2. Add the cold, cubed unsalted butter to the food processor and pulse until the mixture resembles coarse crumbs.
3. Gradually add ice water, 1 tablespoon at a time, and pulse until the dough starts to come together.
4. Turn the dough out onto a floured surface and shape it into a disk. Wrap it in plastic wrap and refrigerate for at least 30 minutes.

Making the Filling:

1. In a large bowl, beat the granulated sugar and eggs together until well combined.
2. Add the heavy cream, whole milk, vanilla extract, ground cinnamon, ground nutmeg, and salt. Mix until smooth.
3. Gently fold in the cooked and mashed butternut squash.

Assembling:

1. Preheat your oven to 350°F (175°C).
2. Roll out the chilled pie crust on a floured surface to fit a 9-inch (23cm) pie dish. Trim any excess dough.
3. Pour the butternut squash filling into the pie crust.

Making the Topping:

1. In a small bowl, combine the chopped walnuts, brown sugar, all-purpose flour, and softened unsalted butter. Mix until it forms a crumbly mixture.
2. Sprinkle the walnut topping evenly over the butternut squash filling.
3. Bake in the preheated oven for 45-50 minutes, or until the pie is set and the top is golden brown.
4. Let the Swiss Thanksgiving Pie cool before serving.

SWISS HANUKKAH LATKES

Servings: 4-6 Time: 30 minutes

Ingredients:

- 4 large russet potatoes, peeled
- 1 medium onion
- 2 large eggs
- 2 tablespoons all-purpose flour
- 1 teaspoon salt
- 1/4 teaspoon black pepper
- Vegetable oil, for frying
- Applesauce and sour cream, for serving

Instructions:

1. Grate the peeled potatoes and onion using the large holes of a box grater or a food processor.
2. Place the grated potatoes and onion in a clean kitchen towel or cheesecloth and squeeze out as much liquid as possible.

3. In a large mixing bowl, combine the squeezed potato and onion mixture with the eggs, all-purpose flour, salt, and black pepper. Mix well.
4. In a large skillet, heat about 1/4 inch (0.5cm) of vegetable oil over medium-high heat.
5. When the oil is hot, carefully drop spoonfuls of the potato mixture into the hot oil, flattening them slightly with the back of a spoon. Be sure not to overcrowd the pan.
6. Fry the latkes until they are golden brown and crispy, about 3-4 minutes per side.
7. Remove the latkes from the skillet and place them on a plate lined with paper towels to drain any excess oil.
8. Serve the Swiss Hanukkah Latkes hot with applesauce and sour cream on the side.

SWISS VALENTINE'S CHOCOLATE FONDUE

Servings: 2-4 Time: 15 minutes

Ingredients:

- 6 ounces (170g) good quality Swiss chocolate (milk, dark, or a mix)
- 1/2 cup (120ml) heavy cream
- 1 teaspoon pure vanilla extract
- A pinch of salt
- Dippers (e.g., strawberries, banana slices, marshmallows, cubes of pound cake)

Instructions:

1. Chop the Swiss chocolate into small, uniform pieces to ensure it melts evenly.
2. In a saucepan over low heat, warm the heavy cream until it starts to steam but is not boiling. Remove it from the heat immediately.
3. Add the chopped chocolate to the warm cream, and let it sit for a minute to soften.
4. Gently stir the mixture until the chocolate is completely melted and the fondue is smooth.
5. Stir in the pure vanilla extract and a pinch of salt.
6. Transfer the chocolate fondue to a fondue pot or a heatproof serving dish that can be kept warm over a tea light or a low flame.
7. Serve the fondue with an assortment of dippers like strawberries, banana slices, marshmallows, and cubes of pound cake.
8. Use fondue forks or wooden skewers to dip the goodies into the warm, velvety chocolate.

MEASUREMENT CONVERSIONS

Volume Conversions:

- 1 cup = 8 fluid ounces = 240 milliliters
- 1 tablespoon = 3 teaspoons = 15 milliliters
- 1 fluid ounce = 2 tablespoons = 30 milliliters
- 1 quart = 4 cups = 32 fluid ounces = 946 milliliters
- 1 gallon = 4 quarts = 128 fluid ounces = 3.78 liters
- 1 liter = 1,000 milliliters = 33.8 fluid ounces
- 1 milliliter = 0.034 fluid ounces = 0.002 cups

Weight Conversions:

- 1 pound = 16 ounces = 453.592 grams
- 1 ounce = 28.349 grams
- 1 gram = 0.035 ounces = 0.001 kilograms
- 1 kilogram = 1,000 grams = 35.274 ounces = 2.205 pounds

Temperature Conversions:

- To convert from Fahrenheit to Celsius: (°F - 32) / 1.8
- To convert from Celsius to Fahrenheit: (°C * 1.8) + 32

Length Conversions:

- 1 inch = 2.54 centimeters
- 1 foot = 12 inches = 30.48 centimeters
- 1 yard = 3 feet = 36 inches = 91.44 centimeters
- 1 meter = 100 centimeters = 1.094 yards
- 1 kilometer = 1,000 meters = 0.621 miles.